George Orwell Studies

Volume Three

No. 1

George Orwell

Publishing Office
Abramis Academic
ASK House
Northgate Avenue
Bury St. Edmunds
Suffolk
IP32 6BB
UK

Tel: +44 (0)1284 700321
Fax: +44 (0)1284 717889
Email: info@abramis.co.uk
Web: www.abramis.co.uk

Copyright
All rights reserved. No part of this publication may be reproduced in any material form (including photocopying or storing it in any medium by electronic means, and whether or not transiently or incidentally to some other use of this publication) without the written permission of the copyright owner, except in accordance with the provisions of the Copyright, Designs and Patents Act 1988, or under terms of a licence issued by the Copyright Licensing Agency Ltd, 33-34, Alfred Place, London WC1E 7DP, UK. Applications for the copyright owner's permission to reproduce part of this publication should be addressed to the Publishers.

© 2018 George Orwell Studies & Abramis Academic

ISSN 2399-1267
ISBN 978-1-84549-734-7

George Orwell

Contents

Special Issue: Orwell and the Arts

Guest Editorial

Examining the 'Genius' of Orwell's Art – by Tim Crook — Page 3

Papers

Keynote: Orwell and Literary Art – by Len Platt — Page 7

'The Art of Donald McGill': Orwell and the Pleasures of Sex – by Richard Lance Keeble — Page 21

Performance and Spectation in Orwell's *Burmese Days* – by Douglas Kerr — Page 37

Orwell, Poetry and the Microphone – by Tim Crook — Page 51

Short Story

2017 My Year of Orwell – and *One Last Gift* – by Nicola Rossi — Page 60

Article

'Room 103': Orwell's Influence on Contemporary Visual Art – by Glenn Ibbitson — Page 70

Other Papers

Orwell and the Appeal of Opium – by Darcy Moore — Page 83

Orwell as Social Patriot – and British Cinema Studies – by Martin Stollery — Page 103

Book Reviews

Elinor Taylor on *The Proletarian Answer to the Modernist Question*, by Nick Hubble; Peter Stansky on *The Duty to Stand Aside:* Nineteen Eighty-Four *and the Wartime Quarrel of George Orwell and Alex Comfort*, by Eric Laursen; John Newsinger on *Under Siege: The Independent Labour Party in Interwar Britain*, by Ian Bullock; Paul Anderson on *Political and Cultural Perceptions of George Orwell: British and American Views*, by Ian Williams, and Nick Hubble on *Hope Lies in the Proles: George Orwell and the Left*, by John Newsinger — Page 118

Exhibition Review

Orwell-inspired museum installation makes for uneasy viewing – by Darcy Moore — Page 135

Editor
Richard Lance Keeble — University of Lincoln

Reviews Editor
Luke Seaber — University College London

Production Editor
Paul Anderson — University of Essex

Editorial Board
Kristin Bluemel	Monmouth University, New Jersey
Tim Crook	Goldsmiths, University of London
Peter Marks	University of Sydney
John Newsinger	Bath Spa University
Marina Remy	Paris Sorbonne
Jean Seaton	University of Westminster
Peter Stansky	Stanford University, US
D. J. Taylor	Author, journalist, biographer of Orwell
Florian Zollmann	Newcastle University

EDITORIAL

Examining the 'Genius' of Orwell's Art

TIM CROOK

The third George Orwell Studies Conference – held at Goldsmiths, University of London, on 30 May 2018 – debated Orwell's status as an artist and how he had inspired others to create art. The themes were varied, covering Orwell's literary art, Orwell and the Spanish Civil War, his influence on artists, Orwell and the art of drama, his essay 'The Art of Donald McGill' and the overall treatment of sex in his writings, the representation of dance in his novel *Burmese Days*, Orwell and the art of propaganda in book covers, his inspiration to new writers – plus Orwell and the art of the microphone. No doubt Orwell himself would have guffawed at such academic attention to his work.

Orwell memorably argued that 'All art is propaganda' (Orwell and Angus 1970: 492) in his seminal 1939 essay on Charles Dickens, though he cleverly added that 'not all propaganda is art'. And he later wrote in his 1946 essay 'Why I Write': 'What I have most wanted to do throughout the last ten years is to make political writing into an art' (ibid: 27). It is significant that Orwell always writes about art not as a grand concept. Orwell's literary appreciation of Dickens, in fact, helped found the 'cultural studies approach' which analyses literary art, crucially, in its political, social and cultural context. Thus, of Dickens' face, he writes:

> It is the face of a man of about forty, with a small beard and a high colour. He is laughing, with a touch of anger in his laughter, but no triumph, no malignity. It is the face of a man who is always fighting against something, but who fights in the open and is not frightened, the face of a man who is generously angry – in other words, of a nineteenth-century liberal, a free intelligence, a type hated with equal hatred by all the smelly little orthodoxies which are now contending for our souls (ibid: 504).

The notion of somebody being generously angry is just one of the deft strokes of Orwell's genius on the canvass of artistic political writing. Indeed, the keynote presentation in the conference by

Len Platt also considered aspects of Orwell's genius. In 'Orwell and Literary Art', Professor Platt addresses the question of whether Orwell was, as one contemporary novelist said, 'a literary mediocrity', or the pioneer of a unique political literary aesthetic. He begins by analysing how Orwell's original analysis of comics (of all things) engaged with his own enthusiastic consumption and appreciation of the genre both as a lad and later on in life.

Orwell's celebrated essay on 'Boys' Weeklies' (1939) argued that comics encouraged 'ordinary' people to fantasise about the education of elites making the public school a 'wildly thrilling and romantic' place that people 'yearn after' and 'day-dream' about. Comics also promoted what Orwell called 'bully-worship and the cult of violence'. Professor Platt observes that his essays 'make us realise that cultural studies existed some time before Raymond Williams or Richard Hoggart could have seriously thought about it and that Orwell was crucial to its development and its ownership on the intellectual left'.

The paper then draws a parallel between James Joyce's *Ulysses* (1922) and the fascinating continuous stream of consciousness play within Orwell's *A Clergyman's Daughter* (1935). Professor Platt is interested in the merging of styles in Orwell's books which makes them complex cultural and literary phenomena and so challenges Will Self's critique of Orwell as a staid and conservative exponent of an old-fashioned version of the English novel.

Richard Lance Keeble next examines the centrality of sex in the Orwellian oeuvre which, he suggests, has been largely missed by critics and biographers. He develops an original thesis that 'explicit homoeroticism' and an 'almost New Mannish frankness about his own sexual history' have gone largely unacknowledged. In particular, Professor Keeble examines Orwell's ground-breaking essay on the saucy seaside postcards of Donald McGill published in Cyril Connolly's literary journal *Horizon* in September 1941. While Keeble acknowledges the feminist critique that Orwell's life and writing could, at times, be described as 'misogynistic', he also argues that he had another side in which he was able to explore and represent his own sexuality with remarkable candour – and even celebrate the pleasures of sex!

Douglas Kerr puts the spotlight on the episode in *Burmese Days* when the central character, Flory, escorts Elizabeth Lackersteen to see a Burmese *pwe* dance, performed in a street in the town of Kyauktada. In 'Performance and Spectation in Orwell's *Burmese Days*', Professor Kerr explains that the English visitors are both spectators of the performance and the crowd, and the objects of curious spectation by the local audience. The *pwe* ritual offers a transformative opportunity to understand 'highbrow and popular

Western ideas of performance, and of the Orient' in the modern age. Significantly, when confronted by the buttock-wiggling of one of the dancers, Elizabeth abruptly leaves. Professor Kerr concludes: 'As the narrow-minded, body-denying, philistine, respectable, ridiculous, spectating bourgeois, she is giving an excellent if unintended performance of the essential fool of modernism.'

2017 was Nicola Rossi's 'Year of Orwell'. Her recognition in The Orwell Society's Student Fiction Competition inspired her to keep on writing and she read to the conference a chapter from her novel, *Rock Star Ending*. As she explained, her prose 'questions whether it is possible for people to tell the difference between choice and manipulation in an increasingly data-driven world'. What are the circumstances that could make 'ordinary people … bring about the premature demise of their fellow human beings?' It is not all gloom and doom. Nicola Rossi also seeks to find out what might inspire them to help each other carry on.

Glenn Ibbitson, in presenting to the conference a paper titled 'Room 103: Orwell's Influence on Contemporary Visual Art', argues that so many visual artists identify with Orwell because his work powerfully advances the principle of the freedom of the individual to think independently. Ibbitson curates an online platform 'Room 103' where artists engaged in visual media can present work inspired by 'Orwellian' themes. And his paper bristles with an Orwellian mischief: 'Now you may justifiably label me as the artist who put the lie in artistic licence and to that charge I plead guilty, but only to the extent that Orwell himself ascribed fictional, nefarious activities to his room on that same corridor. We all crave a catchy title after all.'

Finally, in 'Orwell, Poetry and the Microphone', I examine Orwell's writing aesthetic – particularly as it was applied to his work for radio. Poetry was the style of his first ever published writing when a child. It seems the draft of a poem with the agonising line 'Seven separate pains played in his body like an orchestra' (Venables 2015: 55) was most likely his last ever writing. The publication in 2015 of a volume dedicated to his poems, edited by Dione Venables (with an incisive Preface by the editor and compiler of Orwell's 20-volume *The Complete Works*, Professor Peter Davison, and a book cover endorsement from Orwell's biographer Gordon Bowker), highlighted the importance (too often ignored) of the genre to Orwell throughout his life. In this paper, I argue that Orwell's criticism of poets and poetry, his deliberate attempt to retrieve the oral tradition of poetry in his broadcasting, as well as his own forays into the genre merit a revaluation of Orwell, the writer.

REFERENCES

Venables, Dione (2015) *George Orwell: The Complete Poetry*, England: Finlay Publisher for the Orwell Society

Orwell, Sonia and Angus, Ian (eds) (1970) *The Collected Essays, Journalism and Letters of George Orwell, Volume 1, An Age Like This 1920-1940*, Harmondsworth, Middlesex: Penguin Books

- Richard Lance Keeble adds: John Newsinger, who originally came up with the idea of producing an academic journal devoted to the life and writings of George Orwell, has decided (for personal reasons) to step down from the position of joint editor. I would like to thank him for his tremendous work helping in the launching of the journal, for his incisive peer reviewing and book reviewing – and for sharing his many contacts in the Orwellian world. I am sure his vital contributions will continue in his role as an editorial member. So John: sincere thanks.

PAPER

Orwell and Literary Art

LEN PLATT

This speculative piece is about Orwell's literary reception and notions of cultural value – how it is that some writers achieve status at the highest levels and others, like Orwell, are relegated to a second division. The establishing of such hierarchies in the later twentieth century was often contingent on the making of a distinction between modernist writing, often seen as the highest form of art writing and a unique form of 'art for art's sake', and the purposefulness of writing regarded as lesser – genre writing, journalism, polemic and so on. This essay highlights Orwell's interest in modernist writing and considers what it might mean to think of him in modernist, and postmodernist, terms.

Keywords: Orwell, literary value, modernism

ORWELL, COMICS, LITERARY VALUE – A BRIEF AND PERSONAL HISTORY OF COMICS AND 'LITERATURE'

When people in my line of work talk about Orwell they are usually not very far away from talking about something called 'literature and politics'. In preparing for this paper, I've found myself thinking more directly about Orwell and comics and my own early reading habits. Both have their political dimensions but for the duration of working on this piece the Orwell who wrote about communism has interested me less than the Orwell who wrote about Billy Bunter and the American 'horror and crime' comics. Maybe this is because I now live in a post-communist age where comic book culture has flourished in ways that would have been unthinkable in the 1940s, even for Orwell. But the simpler explanation is probably that I first got to 'literature' by reading comics, as many people must have. Or, to put that in a better way, comics were my first literature. I was born in 1954, but Billy Bunter was still a contemporary figure then, figuring in comics, novels and television shows, and American superheroes were in an ascendency that has proved to be endlessly renewable. From that perspective it is not surprising that, for me, there are 'relations' between comics and Orwell's position in literary art. Precisely what those relations are though will need 'unpacking'.

In 1940, at England's darkest hour, Orwell sat himself down to the task of writing a now famous essay which he entitled 'Boys' Weeklies'. It begins with Orwell in anthropological mode

LEN PLATT

commenting on the ubiquity of comics and magazines and making the assertion, radical in its day, that this throwaway culture rather than, something like, say, *King Lear*, offers the 'best available indication of what the mass of the English people really feels and thinks'. Comics are consumed, Orwell says, across the UK and they are read by all social classes. Except that the educated elites soon outgrow them, moving on to more literary things, while the working classes, he claims, tend not to – retarded in this respect as in others. The focus of the essay is on the school story, a form unique to England and rooted in the class system. 'Ordinary' people fantasise about the education of elites which makes the public school a 'wildly thrilling and romantic' place that people 'yearn after' and 'day-dream' about. The politics of these stories are conservative and characterised by two central elements – 'nothing ever changes' and 'foreigners are funny' (Orwell 1980 [1940]: 484).

Most readers probably remember this part of the essay where Orwell writes about the literary importance of Billy Bunter and the fake public school culture invented by Frank Richards, wrongly assumed by Orwell to be a collective writing under a single name so great was the Bunter story output. But there is another part to the essay where Orwell comments on a different, more modern comic phenomenon located a long way from the 'safe' world of the public school. This kind of comic is technically more accomplished than *The Magnet* or *The Gem*, produced in different ways and characterised not least by being caught up with fantasies about modern science. Above all, especially in the American version, new comic culture becomes associated with what Orwell calls 'bully-worship and the cult of violence' (ibid: 489). In these 'Yank Mags' school boys are asked to identify with 'some variant of Tarzan, with an air ace, a master spy, an explorer, a pugilist – at any rate with some single all-powerful character who dominates everyone about him and whose usual method of solving any problem is a sock on the jaw' (ibid). Orwell goes on: 'You get real blood-lust, really gory descriptions of the all-in, jump-on-his-testicles style of fighting, written in a jargon that has been perfected by people who brood endlessly on violence' (ibid: 488). The connection between the modern incarnation of the comic and the fascist world of the 30s and 40s is made clear. Orwell continues:

> When hatred of Hitler became a major emotion in America, it was interesting to see how promptly 'anti-Fascism' was adapted to pornographic purposes by the editors of the Yank Mags. One magazine which I have in front of me is given up to a long complete story, *When Hell Came to America*, in which the agents of a 'blood-maddened European dictator' are trying to conquer the U.S.A. with death-rays and invisible aeroplanes. There is the frankest appeal to sadism, scenes in which Nazis tie bombs to women's backs and fling them off heights to watch them blown to pieces in mid-air, others in which they tie naked girls together

by their hair and prod them with knives to make them dance, etc., etc. The editor comments solemnly on all this and uses it as a plea for tightening up restrictions against immigrants (ibid: 489).

By the mid-1950s much of the white Anglo-Saxon world was caught up in a moral panic about the same American comic book culture that had so concerned Orwell back in 1940. Everyday comics were now found culpable for just about every social problem – crime, drug addiction, sexual 'perversion', low educational attainment and so on. It was claimed that no fewer than 350 million comics were being sold in the UK every year, 60 million of them being of the offensive American type. So-called 'horror and crime' comics were banned in Sweden in 1949 and in New Zealand in 1954. One year later, activists in England led by the National Council of the Women of Great Britain, the National Union of Teachers and the Anglican Church secured a similar piece of legislation called the Children and Young Person's (Harmful Publications) Act (see Williams 1956: 4-5). The guru of the crusade was Fredric Wertham M. D., American psychologist and interpreter of the dark world of comic book connotation. 'Robin', he wrote in lush tones, 'is a handsome, ephebic boy usually shown in his uniform with bare legs. He is buoyant with energy and devoted to nothing on earth or in interplanetary space as to Bruce Wayne. He often stands with his legs spread, the genital region discreetly evident' (Wertham 1955: 191).

Ten years on. I would have been ten years old in 1964. I did not come from a family rich in conventional literary culture but I did have at least one cultural advantage over the kids that I knew. Comics came to me free, courtesy of my stepfather, Jack Carrington, who possessed a union 'ticket' guaranteeing him work on 'the papers' in the days when they operated from Fleet Street and Farringdon. This gave him access to newspapers and comics in ridiculous quantities. Most kids might get one or perhaps two comics a week. Every day after Jack's night shift, a whole bundle of publications would arrive at our breakfast table. This might include five or six UK newspaper titles; Marvel and DC superhero comics; American funnies like *Sad Sack*, *Casper the Friendly Ghost*, *Richie Rich*, *Little Lotta*, and *Devil Kids, Starring Hot Stuff*; UK staples including *The Beezer*, *The Topper*, *The Beano*, *The Dandy*, *Hotspur*, *Hornet*, *The Boy's Own Paper*, *The Victor*, *The Wizard* and *The Eagle* and the odd compilation of newspaper cartoon strips – annuals by Giles, omnibuses featuring *The Perishers*, *Andy Capp* Year Books, Charles Schultz titles like *You Can Do It Charlie Brown*, *Snoopy Come Home*, *Good Grief Charlie Brown*. And then there was *MAD*, a genuinely subversive publication that gave me an early education in the dark arts of satire, parody and the grotesque. I read comics and comic strips religiously over a period of seven or eight years and made periodic returns after. Those I really liked I collected and curated,

LEN PLATT

placing them in Aristotelian orders of style and form. Others were swapped either with friends or at Comic Exchange shops. There were two of these locally, one at Camberwell the other at New Cross, where the comics you were selling went for next to nothing. Still, their existence made the point that in my world at that time comics were important enough to constitute a kind of currency.

By the 1960s and 1970s liberal education orthodoxies were no longer so exercised about comic book culture. In their reformed versions, comics were not thought to be so bad after all. They were not widely considered to be of any serious cultural value either, but, who knows, they might lead to 'better' things – reading fluency for instance that would somehow take people like me tremulously to the classics of the literary canon. That did not quite happen in my case. I did develop a reading appetite, but not for Shakespeare, Chaucer, the Romantics or the nineteenth-century realist novel. Alongside comics, I read things like Dennis Wheatley, Agatha Christie, H. G. Wells, H. Rider Haggard and more contemporary writers like Isaac Asimov, Arthur C. Clarke, Ian Fleming and more 'literary' material, as long as I considered it 'modern'. I remember reading J. P. Donleavy's *The Ginger Man* when I was around 15, alongside Alan Garner's *The Owl Service* and developed a curious interest in Beckett's plays and the work of other 'absurdists' around the same time. Sometimes this diet seemed strange to others although for me, of course, it was quite normal.

Another few years on into the mid to late 1970s and I was preparing to be examined in material for university entrance. Answering questions on Shakespeare and Chaucer was compulsory, but we (or, rather, our teachers) could choose between writing on authors like Webster, Milton and Fielding. I had no advantage in relation to this kind of material. I did have an advantage though, when it came to Orwell. As a 16-year-old studying at what was then called O level, I was tested on *Animal Farm* and this novel is a kind of cartoon without pictures. I knew all about cartoons. At 18, at A-level, I was examined on the collection *Inside the Whale and Other Essays*. These were political essays and I knew something about those things too, not least from reading counter culture stuff like *MAD*, *OZ* and *The International Times*. Orwell for me then represented a way of articulating with and against the canon at the same time. Here was someone who *was* literary establishment. He had to be. He was on exam syllabuses. But it soon became apparent that he was of a 'different order' to the likes of Dryden and Shakespeare and represented at that time something of a concession to contemporaneity. He might have been an *important* writer, but it was made quite clear that he was not 'top draw'. He did *not* belong to any 'Great Tradition'. He might have been a hugely influential writer, but he was not a great 'literary' novelist.

That kind of positioning of Orwell has never really gone away, although it has had to change its form significantly over the years. From the 1950s through to the 1980s it was routinely argued that Orwell was both 'the conscience of his generation' and a 'saint' and yet *also* second rank – a mere journalist, a didact who failed to live up to top literary standards. The fact that his most famous books, *Animal Farm* and *Nineteen Eighty-Four*, were genre novels meant that they could not be taken that seriously as high literature and for some extremely serious-minded people, that rendered them half-adolescent, like the comics Orwell himself was writing about in the 1940s. Now, some 40 years after the high-water mark of postmodernism, those kind of views are no longer seriously sustainable, at least not among the literati of a major contemporary cultural capital like London. Here the kind of cultural value judgements espoused by the Great Tradition have been systematically dismantled, at least in theory, and the lines once drawn so definitively between high and low culture have, again in theory, been erased as part of that process. So, if someone like Will Self wants to reflate debates about where Orwell sits in the canon he needs to use a different set of terms. Instead of saying that Orwell was a mere journalist, or a didact, rather than a 'real' writer, Self argues that Orwell was merely 'English' in an old-fashioned, parochial kind of way and it is this heavily racialised version of things that makes him forever second-rate and out-of-date (Self 2014). From that kind of perspective, Orwell's alleged insistence on plain writing in 'an unadorned Anglo-Saxon style' becomes ill-informed and worse, indicative of a narrow mindedness that fails to respond to the living vitality of language, and, especially, to cultural diversity. Here the six rules for good writing famously articulated in Orwell's 1946 essay 'Politics and the English Language', at one time read as a defence against cultural 'corruption', become themselves the signs of an ideological intervention – not quite as dangerous as Newspeak maybe but, according to Self, an ideology nonetheless (ibid). 'Orwell and his supporters', claims Self, 'may say they're objecting to jargon and pretension, but underlying this are good old-fashioned prejudices against difference itself. Only homogenous groups of people all speak and write identically. People from different heritages, ethnicities, classes and regions speak the same language differently' (ibid). Self goes on:

> If you want to expose the Orwellian language police for the old-fashioned authoritarian elitists they really are, you simply ask them which variant of English is more grammatically complex – Standard English or the dialect linguists call African American Vernacular English. The answer is, of course, it's the latter that offers its speakers more ways of saying more things – you feel me? (ibid).

LEN PLATT

Actually the truer answer to that question is that no variant is more complex grammatically than another. The real point I want to make though is that here, then, we have two strategies for taking Orwell out of the writing top draw when it comes to literary art – one from the 1950s, the other from the post-postmodern. They take very different routes, but they arrive at more or less the same destination. Whichever way we go, we end up with a species of cultural classification, a hierarchy. If we are talking about modern literature a figure like James Joyce, much admired by Orwell, would appear at the apex of our canon. Orwell himself would feature much lower down, where he features as an anti-modern, not least because of his alleged insistence on the clear, the unambiguous and the straight-talking, as opposed to the ornate, the complex, the overwrought – the 'literary' as we often and most typically understand it. Either way, these kind of views render the idea of Orwell the literary artist highly problematic and, apparently, deeply controversial.

INSIDE 'INSIDE THE WHALE'

What might be invested in this kind of positioning was well said a good few years ago in a book called *The Politics and the Poetics of Transgression* (Stallybrass and White 1986):

> Cultural categories of high and low, social and aesthetic ... but also those of the physical body and geographical space, are never entirely separable. The ranking of literary genres or authors in a hierarchy analogous to social classes is a particularly clear example of a much broader and more complex cultural process whereby the human body, psychic forms, geographical space and the social formation are all constructed within interrelated and dependent hierarchies of high and low.

I want to move on now, away from the politics of reception – or, more precisely, from the issue of how Orwell has been positioned in literary art by cultural elites – to the question of what Orwell himself made of 'literary art' and his own position in it. Firstly, it is worth pointing out that Orwell wrote a great deal about literature – there are many more essays on literature than there are on politics in Orwell. Just to be clear on that, I realise that the phrase 'all literature is political' or something like it, runs like a mantra through Orwell, but it is not difficult to see that something like 'Notes on Nationalism' (1945) is political in a way that the essay titled 'W. B. Yeats' (1943) is not and equally that the latter essay is literary in ways that, say, 'Antisemitism in Britain' (1945) cannot be. In these literary essays as well as writing brilliantly on Yeats, Orwell wrote brilliantly on Dickens. He also wrote on Charles Reade, Mark Twain, Arthur Koestler, Tolstoy, Kipling (again brilliantly) and Wells (also brilliantly) and many more. In addition to all that there were countless allusions to a huge range of writers and their texts spread across the whole essay output as well as in the letters and the reviews. Read across this body of work and it becomes clear that Orwell, like the rest of us, has his favourites but he never seems much interested in the maintenance of canonical order and the pieties of hierarchy. He writes about canonical writers for sure, but he is equally happy writing about 'popular' culture. 'Raffles and Miss Blandish' (1944), for example, compares end-of-century detective fiction with 1930s noir.

He also wrote on such things as music hall, once stating that he would much rather have written the lyrics to the music-hall song 'Two Lovely Black Eyes' than Rosetti's poem 'The Blessed Damozel' or Meredith's 'Love in the Valley' (Orwell 2000 [1945]: 321). He wrote, too, on nonsense poetry and seaside postcards. In this respect Orwell's essays is like reading cultural studies *avant la lettre*. His interest is not in establishing the qualities of great literature, but in understanding the historical and political contexts that produce literary cultures of all kinds. That does not mean, however, that he is uninterested in aesthetics. In fact he returns to the idea of aesthetics over and over again in his essays. But he constructs aesthetics in, or rather as, a historical and political domain, and this is one reason why we still read these essays today. They make us realise that cultural studies existed some time before Raymond Williams or Richard Hoggart could have seriously thought about it and that Orwell was crucial to its development, and its ownership on the intellectual left.

One obvious place to see Orwell's engagement with literary aesthetics and his sense of their connection with the political, is in the title essay of that collection of essays I was examined on in 1972, 'Inside the Whale'. I never thought so then but this is a fascinating piece. It starts out as a review of Henry Miller's novel *Tropic of Cancer* which was published in 1935 to great controversy over its alleged pornographic content, although it soon becomes clear that Orwell is not that interested in the pornography debate and that *Tropic of Cancer* is really just the starting point for an essay that has a much more ambitious range and scope. The real purpose of 'Inside the Whale' is to offer up a historiographical map which attempts to impose some kind of shape and order on high-end literary culture as it appeared from around 1900 to 1939. The main emphasis is on distinguishing what Orwell takes to be a major fault line separating out the 1920s from the 1930s.

> [I]n the years 1930-1935, something happens. The literary climate changes .... Suddenly, we have got out of the twilight of the gods into a sort of Boy Scout atmosphere of bare knees and community singing. The typical literary man ceases to be a cultured expatriate with a leaning towards the Church, and becomes an eager-minded schoolboy with a leaning towards Communism (Orwell 1962 [1940]: 29-30).

The former period is characterised by a group of writers that, as Orwell points out, were never really a group at all. It includes, in Orwell's formulation, such figures as Anaïs Nin, T. S. Eliot, Ezra Pound, Wyndham Lewis and, of course, Miller and Joyce. We now think of these writers as 'modernists' but that term never existed in that way in the 1920s and these writers articulated no common agenda. The 1930s are characterised by a new wave comprised of such figures as Stephen Spender, Christopher Isherwood, W. H. Auden and Louis MacNeice. These did see themselves very much as a group. Indeed they used the 1932 collection *New Signatures*, edited by Michael Roberts, and MacNeice's book *Modern Poetry: A Personal Essay* (1938) to set out an agenda, a specific *riposte* in fact to the writers of the earlier period. They construct themselves explicitly as political activists writing against an old guard of worn-out dilettantes and aesthetes.

A large part of 'Inside the Whale' is devoted to characterising what Orwell sees as the differences between this 'old guard' (the modernists) and the 'new wave' and with historicising how those differences may have come about. A schematic might summarise those differences with the terms 'ornate', 'everyday', 'detached', 'commonplace', 'interior', 'obscene', 'apolitical' or 'towards fascism' on one side, representing the 1920s, and, for the new wave, 'serious', 'engaged',' partisan', 'left', 'anti-fascist', 'purposeful'. Now, I don't know a single specialist in the literature of this period who could swallow whole this version of things. Most would probably strongly object to every single element of it in fact, because that's what specialists do with such schemas. But the question of whether Orwell is right or wrong about this particular piece of literary history is not really the point. The interest is in the qualitative judgements that he makes about the writing of these decades. The modernists have high status. These are writers seemingly indifferent to the pressing issues of the day and devoted to apparently meaningless ephemera. Miller's *Tropic of Cancer*, is totally detached from the big political issues. As Orwell points out, it contains no reference at all to, say, Mussolini marching into Abyssinia nor to Hitler's concentration camps which were beginning to appear in the 1930s. And yet it is precisely this modernist aesthetic of the everyday that Orwell wants to elevate. The truly remarkable thing for Orwell is 'the commonplaceness of its material'. (ibid: 11). The 'real achievement', he writes, is to have the sheer daring to write about 'the stuff' which is 'under everybody's nose' and which is supposed to be largely 'incommunicable' – the 'recognisable experiences of human beings' (ibid: 11-12). 'Why are these … monstrous trivialities so engrossing?' (ibid: 13).

> Simply because the whole atmosphere is deeply familiar, because you have all the while the feeling that this is really happening to *you*. And you have this feeling because somebody has chosen to

drop the Geneva language of the ordinary novel and drag the *real-politik* of the inner mind into the open (ibid).

Notice in that statement the phrase condemning literary bureaucracy and the counter comment about devices like interior monologue or stream of consciousness bringing a '*real-politik* of the inner mind into the open' – a telling illustration of the old cliché that the private is the political. This kind of literature might be art literature and insiderly in various ways, but it is *not*, for Orwell, *outside* of history and politics – even though it claims detachment and seems indifferent. It is, on the contrary, inside the minutiae of the politics of everyday experience and that makes it somehow 'real'. Here in contrast, is what he writes about political commitment and the writers of the 30s:

> [These writers] fit easily into the public-school-university-Bloomsbury pattern. [They are the products of a new orthodoxy that] made a certain set of opinions absolutely *de rigueur* on certain subjects ... To people of that kind such things as purges, secret police, summary executions, imprisonments without trial etc., etc., are too remote to be terrifying. They can swallow totalitarianism *because* they have no experience of anything except liberalism .... So much of-left wing thought is playing with fire by people who don't even realise the fire is hot (ibid: 30).

So the writers of the 1930s essentially fail because their version of politics is a fantasy produced not least by a privileged life in the soft, liberal culture of England. The writers of the 1920s, however, are, first, much less socially homogenous. Quite a few are émigrés – one is Irish, one American, one was born in Canada – one is working-class, several are women and one of those was born of Cuban parents in France. These writers are able to anatomise modern life from within, not least because of what Orwell calls 'the bourgeois liberty' without which 'creative powers' will wither away under political repression and orthodoxy (ibid: 39). Modernism, then, the literature of innovation and experimentation, for Orwell represents the continuation, and the allowance, of a *true* literary tradition and there is no doubt that he identifies with it. 'Good novels,' he says 'are not written by orthodoxy-sniffers, nor by people who are conscience-stricken about their own unorthodoxy. Good novels are written by people who are *not frightened*' (ibid: 40). That statement opens the way to thinking about Orwell not in relation to those 'political' English writers of the 1930s like Auden and Isherwood but rather in relation to figures such as Joyce and Miller with whom Orwell identified so strongly. Given what Orwell says in 'Inside the Whale', is there any mileage in thinking about him as a modernist writer, then, or stranger still, a writer who points the way towards postmodern aesthetics in some respects?

LEN PLATT

Maybe, but for now I want to emphasise that 'Inside the Whale' is deeply counter intuitive. It seriously inverts what we might have expected were Orwell really a 'political' thinker first, as many have contended, and a 'literary' writer second. And there is a further implication. The dismissal of Auden and co. is strategic. It means that for Orwell, the 1930s had not been *done* by literature in the way that modernism had *done* for the 1920s. That leaves space, of course, for a 'real' political literature which comes out of a real aesthetic based, as it must be in Orwell's view, on a genuine experience of 'ordinary' life. This, I think, helps in reading Orwell, and throws some light on another famous essay of his, 'Why I Write' where he makes this intriguing statement: 'What I have most wanted to do throughout the past ten years is to make political writing into art' (1970 [1946]: 27).

MODERNIST ORWELL?

In this final section, I want to make some suggestions as to what it might mean to read Orwell as a practitioner of 'literary art'. Can we get anywhere with that claim? Do we need to? Some people think so. Quite a few have formulated Orwell in terms of his apparently problematic relation to the Great Tradition, seeking ways to somehow reposition him so that he sits more comfortably amongst the literary elite. Some critics have argued that Orwell's real artistic achievement is rooted not in the genre novels but in the more conventional narratives, the social satires of the 1920s and 30s – such as *Burmese Days* (1933), *Keep the Aspidistra Flying* (1936) and *Coming Up for Air* (1939). These, it has been claimed, are much better novels than we usually give Orwell credit for. Another approach, more well-known, argues that, novelist or not, Orwell is a greater writer by virtue of his *political* essays and that these, whatever else they do, should assure Orwell's place in the top division. Bernard Crick (1980), for instance, argued in that way, although he was not the first to do so, and more recently, so has Jeremy Paxman (2015). Note that neither of these approaches takes real issue with the idea of the Great Tradition, only with the details of who is in and who is excluded.

Do we still need to make these kinds of tortuous argument when it's just as *de rigueur* now to 'deconstruct' the idea of the literary canon as it once was to defend it? In some senses that question closes down the space for a revaluation of Orwell as a literary writer – but in other ways it opens things up. If the divisions between 'high' and 'low' really have become blurred and the boundaries between autobiography, journalism and the fictive really more fluid then we are better positioned to think of Orwell in more contemporary ways.

Let me elaborate on what that means by going back to literary modernism and the ways it was typically formulated by readers in its heyday. Many people, like Orwell himself, were struck firstly by what seemed the startling innovation of interior monologue or 'stream of consciousness'. But if we take again a classic of modernism, Joyce's *Ulysses*, less than one third of that book is written in an interior style. The rest of this remarkable text is made up of all sorts of things. It contains a play, for instance, a history of the novel, a chapter written in a musical style, journalism, a chapter written in an encyclopaedia style, another written like a romance novel and so on. Some of it is thought to be autobiographical and, these days, people join in with Orwell and think it deeply political too.

This hugely influential version of the novel is substantially concerned with appropriating other kinds of material to itself quite outside of realist narrative. That is its hallmark, part of what makes it modernist as well a part of what makes it 'Irish'. To put that another way, its modernism is in part destructive. It takes the social realist novel, a form uniquely associated with England, and mashes it up – like a collage in style terms. This, in fact, has become an aesthetic strategy inextricably linked both to modernism and what followed it into our own contemporary lives. That merging of styles is now generally reckoned to be a much more significant marker of literary modernism than stream-of-consciousness.

The point I want to make at the end of this piece is that it's possible, and might be useful, to think about Orwell as someone working in this kind of tradition – not as a contributor to a staid, conservative, English version of the novel as Will Self insists, but, rather, as a more driven cultural innovator tied in in various ways to modernist literary aesthetic.

If, instead of anatomising Orwell as part journalist, or part essayist, part second-rate novelist we think of him as an innovator, we might find an Orwell placed in new relations to what we often think of as 'literary art'. To do that we need to think of works like *Down and Out in Paris and London* and *The Road to Wigan Pier* less in terms of political journalism or sociology and more in relation to Truman Capote's *In Cold Blood* (1966) and Hunter S. Thompson's *Fear and Loathing in Las Vegas* (1971), texts which, it could be argued, draw on Orwell to challenge and problematise our sense of the separateness of the domains of fact and fictive. We need to focus more than we usually do on the stranger aesthetic demands of Orwell's work. In this context it becomes interesting that a novel like *A Clergyman's Daughter* (1935) contains a long chapter in the middle, representing some fifth of the whole book, which is, in fact, a play. Here that novel again reflects back on Orwell's reading of Joyce's *Ulysses,* a text which did precisely the same thing some thirteen years previously. Here is a short illustration from the beginning of Joyce's version of things:

BLOOM: What is that? A flasher. Searchlight.

(He stands at Comack's corner, watching)

BLOOM: Aurora borealis or a steel foundry? Ah, the brigade, of course. South side anyhow. We're safe. Might be his house. Beggar's bush. We're safe *(He hums cheerfully)*. London's burning, London's burning! On fire, on fire! *(He catches sight of a navvy lurching through the crowd at the farther side of Talbot Street)*. I'll miss him. Run. Quick. Better cross here.

(He darts to cross the road. Urchins shout.)

THE URCHINS: Mind out, mister! *(Two cyclists, with lighted paper lanterns aswing, swim by him, grazing him, their bells rattling.)*

THE BELLS: Haltyaltyaltyall.(Joyce 1940 [1922]: 566).

And this is from *A Clergyman's Daughter*:

Scene: Trafalgar Square. Dimly visible through the mist, a dozen people, Dorothy among them, are grouped about the benches near the north parapet.

CHARLIE [*singing*]: 'Ail Mary, ail Mary, 'ail Mary,'a-il Ma-ry - (Big Ben strikes ten).

SNOUTER [*mimicking the noise*]: Ding dong, ding dong! Shut your – noise can't you? Seven more hours of it on this – square before we get the chance of a setdown and a bit of sleep! Cripes!

MR TALLBOYS [*to himself*]: *Non sum qualis eram boni sub regno Edwardi*! In the days of my innocence, before the Devil carried me up into a high place and dropped me in the Sunday newspapers – that is to say when I was Rector of Little Fawley-cum-Dewsbury (Orwell 1976 [1935]: 343).

This is much more than the appropriation of a device. Both visual and aural landscapes echo each other and both draw on associations between night-time, the unconscious, social and sexual scandal, shame and so on. The geographical transference of Dublin's nighttown to Trafalgar Square becomes a kind of homage, not just to Joyce but to the literary culture he represents.

Reading Orwell as a modernist means also that we should focus on the strange duality of something like *Homage to Catalonia* (1937) which is self-consciously two texts running side by side, one a personal account, the other a political analysis which we are told, in a typically modernist ploy, we can ignore if we're not interested.

Animal Farm too becomes an innovative text read in a modernist/postmodern frame. Forget the politics of book, just for a minute – this is a kind of text now familiar to us in contemporary literary culture. It writes to postmodernism in a formal sense, and to magic realism which was once a dominant species of postmodernism. *Nineteen Eighty-Four* (1949) likewise can be read as a stylistically innovative novel. It might not be the first dystopia but it has been crucial to the development of that form, a form which continues to have a great deal of mileage and currency in contemporary culture and has found itself appropriated by such populist styles as manga and steam punk, one reason why Orwell's text still has such extraordinary life in it. *Nineteen Eighty-Four* also contains at least one aesthetic oddity, a book within a book which purports to be a brilliant revolutionary attack on the totalitarian state but which is most likely to have come from within totalitarianism itself, a system which knows its own corruption better than any outsiderly perspective possibly could. That complex interruption not only breaks the flow of narrative order, it also raises issues of authorship and authenticity which likewise have been fundamental to modernism and later aesthetic cultures.

I could go on making these kinds of adjustments to reading Orwell. The point is only partly to challenge Self's idea that Orwell is a conventional writer whose ordinariness is measured by his apparent 'Englishness'. It should be clear that, in my view, Orwell is much better than that, although at the same time I want to stress that none of what I have written above is designed to make Orwell a writer whom we can now safely slip into the upper ranks of things. On the contrary, there is a great deal to be gained in Orwell's outsiderly status in this respect as Orwell's continuing high-cultural status on the margins indicates. At the same time, however, there may be some mileage to be gained in positioning Orwell in a cultural order wider than the ones usually held to have produced him, beyond public schools and the BBC, even, maybe, beyond the Spanish Civil War – this would be an aesthetically radical context, a challenging cultural disorder that had a fundamental impact on the way Orwell approached writing and the idea of literary art and also, I suspect, on the way he did, or couldn't do, 'politics'.

REFERENCES

Crick, Bernard (1980) *George Orwell: A Life*, London: Secker & Warburg

Joyce, James (1940 [1922]) *Ullyses*, London: Bodley Head

Orwell, George (1976 [1935]) *A Clergyman's Daughter*, *Collected Novels*, London: Secker & Warburg pp 253-426

Orwell, George (1980 [1940]) Boys' Weeklies, *George Orwell*, London: Secker & Warburg/Octopus pp 477-491; originally published in *Inside the Whale and Other Essays*, London: Victor Gollancz, 1940

Orwell, George (1962 [1940]) Inside the Whale, *Inside the Whale and Other Essay*, Harmondsworth, Middlesex: Penguin pp 9-50

LEN PLATT

Orwell, George (2000 [1945]) Good bad books, *George Orwell: Essays*, Harmondsworth, Middlesex: Penguin in association with Secker & Warburg

Orwell, George (1970 [1946]) Why I Write, Orwell, Sonia and Angus, Ian (eds) *The Collected Essays, Journalism and Letters, Vol. 1: An Age Like This*, Harmondsworth, Middlesex: Penguin Books pp 23-30

Paxman, Jeremy (2015) The genius of George Orwell, *Daily Telegraph*, 21 January. Available online at https://www.telegraph.co.uk/culture/books/5453633/The-genius-of-George-Orwell.html

Self, Will (2014) Why Orwell was a literary mediocrity, *A Point of View*, BBC Radio 4, 31 August. Available online at https://www.bbc.co.uk/news/magazine-28971276

Stallybrass, Peter and White, Allon (1986) *The Politics and Poetics of Transgression*, New York: Cornell University Press

Wertham, Fredric (1955) *Seduction of the Innocent*, London: Museum

Williams, Mrs G. E. B. (1956) *An Account of the Work of the National Council of Women of Great Britain on Children's and Horror Comics*, London: National Council of Women of Great Britain

NOTE ON THE CONTRIBUTOR

Len Platt is Professor of Modern Literatures at Goldsmiths College, London. He has published widely on modernist and postmodernist literary cultures, especially on the works of James Joyce and on contemporary culture in various genres and technological forms. His major interest is in the politics of text and the ways culture performs in politically strategic ways. He is also a leading expert on early musical theatre and the exchange and transfer practices that made it a characteristic culture of conservative popular modernism at the turn of the nineteenth century. His most recent book is *Writing London and the Thames Estuary 1576-2016*, an application of centre/margin debates to local geographies of cities and their suburbs.

'The Art of Donald McGill':
Orwell and the Pleasures of Sex

RICHARD LANCE KEEBLE

*The centrality of sex in the writings of George Orwell has been largely missed by critics and biographers. Feminist critics such as Daphne Patai (1984) and Beatrice Campbell (1984) have accused Orwell of misogyny: rightly so. But as so often with Orwell (his character so complex and contradictory) there is another side which this paper will attempt to outline. It will aim to highlight briefly the place of sex in a selection of his works (*Down and Out in Paris and London, Homage to Catalonia*, 'Such, Such were the Joys', Nineteen Eighty-Four). In particular, it will focus on Orwell's (largely unacknowledged) explicit homoeroticism and his almost New Mannish frankness about his own sexual history. Analysis of* Nineteen Eighty Four *will show that the representation of Julia, who conducts a secret affair with the anti-hero Winston Smith, is far more nuanced than generally thought: Orwell lays quite a few hints that she is, indeed, a Party spy drawing Smith into a honeytrap. The paper will move on to consider Orwell's remarkable 1941* Horizon *essay on McGill's sexy seaside postcards. Like Orwell's essays and journalism on turned-up trouser legs, the common toad, cups of tea, boys' weeklies, pubs, Woolworth's roses, handwriting, common lodging houses and trashy American crime novels, this one is brilliantly original in challenging the expectations of his readers: directing his critical gaze at a manifestation of popular culture normally ignored. Orwell mixes attitudes of pleasure (captured, above all, in the humour of the sexy cartoons and his own writing) and* faux *shame. In the process, he explores with a lightness of touch such issues as the essential purpose of jokes, the notion of goodness, gender stereotypes – and the complexities of the human condition, no less.*

Keywords: Donald McGill, irony, Orwell, pleasure, sex, shame

> Susan Watson recalled that when Orwell invited Aunt Nellie Limouzin – wrapped in black satin and adorned with jet beads – to tea in Canonbury Square, he'd amuse her with his collection of postcards by Donald McGill. He told her not to serve tea until Nellie had finished laughing at the jokes (Meyers 2000: 268).

RICHARD LANCE KEEBLE

THE FEMINIST CRITIQUE

The feminist critique of Orwell is, in many respects, persuasive. On his first novel, Urmila Seshagiri (2001: 111) argues: 'The life narratives of women in *Burmese Days* demonstrate that Orwell not only naturalizes but actively deploys misogyny to increase his critique of imperialism' (see also Bluemel 2012: 24; Beddoe 1984). According to Daphne Patai, author of the seminal *The Orwell Mystique: A Study in Male Ideology* (1984), Orwell cultivated 'a traditional notion of masculinity, complemented by a generalized misogyny' (ibid: 15). He 'polarizes human beings according to sex roles and gender identity and legitimizes male displays of dominance and aggression' (ibid: 17). In his journalism, he repeatedly displays his misogyny. For instance, in a review of a novel by Joseph Conrad, he comments: 'One of the surest signs of his genius is that women dislike his books' (ibid: 18). In *Down and Out in Paris and London* (1933), Orwell tends 'to treat men as individuals and women as mere representatives of the inferior female sex' (ibid: 65). In *The Road to Wigan Pier* (1937), his homophobia is manifest 'in the ease with which he attached the label of "pansy" or "Nancy boy" to men he perceived as opponents' (ibid: 85). On *A Clergyman's Daughter* (1935), Patai comments:

> The very title of Orwell's second novel at once induces the reader to take a particular perspective on his protagonist. She is to be viewed not as an individual in her own right but rather in terms of her relationship to a man, a clergyman, her father (ibid: 96).

In *Homage to Catalonia* (1938), his account of his experiences fighting with the Republican militia in Spain, war is represented essentially as a 'masculine initiation rite' (ibid: 140-153).

According to Beatrice Campbell (1984: 129), women simply 'do not appear as protagonists in Orwell's working class'. On *Nineteen Eighty-Four*, she comments: 'Julia is Winston's sleeping partner in sedition. Her rebellion is essentially sexual. She's promiscuous, she's had hundreds of men and her subversion is sealed in an equation between corruption and sexuality.' This reduction of Julia to her corrupt biology renders her rebellion 'as something seething below the threshold of political consciousness' (ibid). For Christopher Hitchens, hardly noted as a feminist, (2002: 105): 'Every one of the female characters [in his novels] is practically devoid of the least trace of intellectual or reflective capacity.' And in his study of Orwell and religion, Michael G. Brennan highlights the way in which he generally ignored the many thousands of middle class and working class Catholic women in England, concentrating, rather, his 'anti-Church ire upon an unrepresentative metropolitan male elite of (often convert) Roman Catholics whose writings and public utterances so irritated him' (2017: xvii-xviii).

Along with Orwell's representation of gender issues, his behaviour, sadly, could also at times be described as misogynistic. In a letter to a relative in 1972, Jacintha Buddicom, a childhood friend of the then-Eric Blair, wrote: 'How I wish I had been ready for betrothal when Eric asked me to marry him on his return from Burma [in 1927]. He had ruined what had been such a close and fulfilling relationship since childhood by trying to take us the whole way before I was anywhere near ready for that' (Davison 2010: 9, cited in Bluemel 2012: 19). Bluemel (ibid) suggests that this substantiates the claim by Dione Venables, in a 'Postscript' to the reprint of Buddicom's memoir *Eric and US: A Remembrance of George Orwell* (2006 [1974]: 182), that he had come close to raping Buddicom. Biographer Bernard Crick also tells of the occasion in 1944 when Orwell accompanied a former BBC acquaintance home late one night after a party at William and Hetta Empson's house in Hampstead, north London, and while crossing the Heath, tried 'to make love to her far too persistently, somewhat violently even' (Crick 1980: 465). A few months later, Orwell made a 'vigorous pass' at Anne Popham (later to wed the art historian, Quentin Bell) while he sat beside her on a bed in an Islington flat. Crick reports (ibid: 485) that Orwell 'said that he was very attracted to her, kissed her and asked if she would consider marrying him. Touched and flattered, though embarrassed and a little shocked by his dispassionate precipitancy, she disengaged herself…'. Later, he sent Popham two letters, not apologising but trying to explain his actions. In the first he wrote: 'It is only that I feel so desperately alone sometimes…' (ibid).[1]

In his biography of Orwell, Robert Colls lists his possible sexual relationships (2013: 292):

> As well as the prostitutes of Burma, Paris, London and Marrakech there is a leading group of other contenders including Jacintha Buddicom, Brenda Salkeld, Eleanor Jaques [Colls has her incorrectly as Jacques], Mabel Fierz [Colls has her incorrectly as Friez], Rosalind Obermeyer. Kay Walton, Sally Jerome, Stevie Smith, Lydia Jackson, Inez Holden, Celia Paget, Ruth Graves, Anne Popham, Audrey Jones, Sally McEwan and Orwell's second wife Sonia Brownell. From what we know of these women and their relationship with Orwell, if they were sexual partners we can be sure they were not only sexual partners.

Colls goes on to suggest that, while it was said Eileen had her flings, 'if she did they seem not to have been nearly so numerous nor so speculative as his' (ibid: 199). John Newsinger is also very critical of Orwell's attitudes to women. He writes (2018: 154): 'He regularly dismissed both "feminists" and "feminism". He was unfortunately one of those male socialists who were opposed to every oppression, except that of women.'

RICHARD LANCE KEEBLE

BUT THEN: THE OTHER SIDE OF ORWELL

Orwell was a complex man with many sides to his personality. And one was distinctly 'un-misogynistic'. This is perhaps not surprising: his mother, Ida (née Limouzin) was a feminist and his aunt Nellie (with whom he stayed occasionally while investigating the plight of the poor in London in the late 1920s and in the early 1930s when she moved to Paris) was to marry Eugène Adam, an ex-anarchist, Esperantist and founder member of the French Communist Party (Brennan 2017: 25). As Brennan comments (ibid: 5):

> Ida and Nellie, and sometimes their eldest sister Norah who had also returned to England, attended Suffragette meetings, concerts and theatres in London. They moved within Fabian circles, mixing with H. G. Wells, G. K. Chesterton and E. E. Nesbit, the author of *The Ballads and Lyrics of Socialism* as well as *The Railway Children*. The radical Christian socialist Conrad le Despenser Roden Noel, the 'Red Vicar' of Thaxted, was at that time the curate of Nellie's local parish in Paddington.

Many of the women Orwell was later to be associated with (Jacintha Buddicom, Stevie Smith, Inez Holden, Mabel Fierz, Celia Kirwan – not to mention his two wives Eileen O'Shaughnessy and Sonia Brownell) were forceful characters who would hardly have tolerated a misogynist. Yet, as Bluemel points out, in the writings of many of them 'there is hardly a mention of feminism, even as these same writings often show sensitivity to women's sexual dependency and their consequently diminished access to well-paid work, accumulated wealth, and assured comfort' (Bluemel 2012: 21).

As a father to Richard Horatio, whom he and Eileen adopted in June 1944, Orwell certainly confounded the expectations of his day, displaying considerable affection for the child, taking him for walks in the pram – and even changing his nappies (though with a cigarette in his mouth). As Crick records on a visit to Arthur and Mamaime Koestler's house near Blaenau Ffestiniog in Merionethshire, Wales, at Christmas 1945:

> There were long walks that Christmas. Orwell would carry Richard along on his hip and Celia [Kirwan, Mamaime's twin sister] noticed how competently he coped with the little boy, bathing him and changing him as if to the manner born, relaxed and unanxious about him – practical activities very unusual in fathers of his generation (Crick 1980: 483).

In the field of domestic politics, Orwell also displayed distinctly progressive (almost New Mannish!) attitudes. For instance, while engaged in his researches into poverty in the north of England (later published in *The Road to Wigan Pier* in 1937), he stayed in

Sheffield with the Searles family. In his diary for 5 March 1936, he records (Orwell and Angus 1970 Vol. 1: 222):

> We had an argument one evening in the Searles' house because I helped Mrs S. with the washing up. Both of the men disapproved of this, of course. Mrs S. seemed doubtful. She said that in the North working class men never offered any courtesies to women (women are allowed to do all the housework unaided, even when the man is unemployed and it is always the man who sits in the comfortable chair) and she took this state of things for granted, but did not see why it should not be changed.

Orwell goes on to identify the gender politics at work in the kitchen and how simply doing the washing up while unemployed could damage a man's sense of his own masculinity – and how, paradoxically, this was accepted by women: 'I think it is instinctively felt by both sexes that the man would lose his manhood if, merely because he was out of work, he became a "Mary Ann"' (ibid).

SEXUALITY AND *DOWN AND OUT*

In the seminal *Slumming: Sexual and Social Politics in Victorian London* (2004), Seth Koven examines how a wide range of clergymen, journalists, novelists, philanthropists, social investigators and reformists in late nineteenth century Britain ventured into poor areas – particularly in London. Koven argues that 'the widely shared imperative among well-to-do men and women to traverse class boundaries and befriend their outcast brothers and sisters in the slums was somehow bound up in their insistent eroticization of poverty and their quest to understand their own sexual subjectivities' (ibid: 4).Orwell was following a long line of socially-concerned writers (such as Jack London, James Greenwood, Charles Booth, Beatrice Potter) when between 1928 and 1931 he went 'down and out' and lived alongside the beggars and hop pickers. Significantly, his celebrated account of his experiences, the part fiction/part memoir *Down and Out in Paris and London* (1933) features sexuality prominently. The account begins with Charlie, a fellow Parisian down-and-out, boasting (somewhat offensively) of his sexual exploits, raping a prostitute in a brothel: 'Without another word I pulled her off the bed and threw her onto the floor. And then I fell upon her like a tiger! … More and more savagely I renewed the attack. Again and again the girl tried to escape, she cried out for mercy anew, but I laughed at her' (Orwell 1980 [1933]: 19).

One of the most remarkable aspects of the book, somewhat underplayed in critiques of the text to date, is the way in which homosexuality is treated so openly: this at a time when it was illegal and taboos hindered any serious discussion of the subject. While staying overnight at a spike in London, Orwell describes how a man began making 'homosexual attempts' upon him (ibid: 86). Orwell adds: 'He was a feeble creature and I could manage him easily, but of course it was impossible to go to sleep again. For the rest of the night we stayed awake, smoking and talking. … Homosexuality is general among tramps of long standing, he said' (ibid). Later, when reflecting on his experiences, Orwell argues that one of the 'great evils' of the tramp's life is that he is cut off entirely from contact with women (ibid: 115). He continues:

> It is obvious what results of this must be: homosexuality, for instance, and occasional rape cases. …The sexual impulse, not to put it any higher, is a fundamental impulse, and starvation of it can be almost as demoralizing as physical hunger (ibid: 116).

HOMAGE TO CATALONIA AND HOMOEROTICISM

Traditionally warfare is often seen as a site for male bonding (Keeble 2015a). Indeed, *Homage to Catalonia* (1962 [1938]), Orwell's account of his time spent fighting alongside Republican militiamen during the Spanish civil war in 1937, begins with a description of a meeting at the Lenin barracks in Barcelona with an Italian soldier which, it could be argued, has a remarkably overt homoerotic element (Keeble 2015b: 213). As he looks intensely at the man, Orwell is fascinated by his violence: he was 'a tough-looking youth of twenty-five or six, with reddish-yellow hair and powerful shoulders. His peaked leather cap was pulled fiercely over one eye … Something in his face deeply moved me' (op cit: 7). The dramatic narrative then shifts to greater intimacy: first they engage in awkward, clipped dialogue – and then the scene comes to a sort of climax as the men's hands touch: 'As we went out he stepped across the room and gripped my hand very hard' (ibid). Orwell reflects: 'Queer, the affection you can feel for a stranger!' This generalisation serves two purposes (Keeble 2015b: 213). From the isolated incident, Orwell is able to draw out an observation about the human predicament and at the same time avoid the personal voice. Perhaps Orwell felt a certain embarrassment/shame about the intensity of feelings for the stranger. He goes on to say, somewhat sadly, that he was never to see the Italian militiaman again. And moving on to an impersonal, generalised 'one' voice (as if to protect himself from pain), while stressing how much that kind of male bonding was a constant feature of life fighting, he comments: 'One was always making contacts of that kind in Spain' (op cit: 7). Indeed, the intensity of the feeling for the Italian was so strong for Orwell that he later in 1939 celebrated the meeting in a poem, 'The Italian soldier shook my hand', which ends movingly: "But the thing that I saw in your face/No power can disinherit:/No bomb that ever burst/Shatters the crystal spirit."[2] Earlier, in Burma (from 1922-1927), attractive boys had been of sexual interest to Eric Blair, according to John Sutherland (2016: 98-99):

He was, he recalled later, attracted by the androgynous beauty of the dominant Burmese race – the 'Burman'. He came to relish the attentions of his young native servants ('boys') when they handled his naked body 'intimately' while bathing and dressing him. Their male bodies, golden, not boiled-beef red, were not disfigured by pubic hair (how did he know that?).

Orwell's ambivalent attitudes towards homosexuality appear in his response to Oscar Wilde. Kristian Williams points out how Orwell expressed in his writings and letters his disdain for 'Nancy poets', 'pious sodomites' and the 'pansy left' (2017: 41). Yet, throughout his life, Orwell had a high opinion of Wilde's writings. Among the last books he read while confined to a sanatorium were two accounts of Wilde's trials and his prison letter, 'De Profundis' (ibid: 42). Williams comments astutely: 'Chief among the commonalities between Orwell and Wilde are their recognition of the value of aesthetics and their opposition to all forms of Puritanism' (ibid: 43).

'SUCH, SUCH WERE THE JOYS' (AND SORROWS) OF SEX!

Orwell's (partly fictionalised) memoir of his time at St Cyprian's prep school, near Eastbourne, between 1911 and 1917, 'Such, Such Were the Joys' (1970 [1952]) is remarkable for the explicitness of the sexual content (Keeble 2018). At the start of Section IV, for instance, there is a lengthy discussion of sex and homosexuality in particular. Sex becomes linked with secrecy, betrayal, ignorance, confusion and shame. Earlier, he had reported how he had 'sneaked' to his favourite teacher, Brown 'a suspected case of homosexuality' (1970 [1952]: 401). He continues: 'I did not know very well what homosexuality was, but I knew that it happened and was bad, and this was one of the contexts in which it was proper to sneak. Brown told me I was a "good fellow" – which made me feel horribly ashamed' (ibid: 401-402). All this leads to a remarkably frank account (how true, how fictional?) of his own sex life and of the sexual development of youths in general. Orwell was never much impressed by psychoanalysis, as biographer Gordon Bowker stresses (Bowker 2003: 48). Yet, if being open about one's feelings and sexuality (making the personal political) is another mark of today's New Man, then Orwell was well ahead of his times (Keeble 2018: 85). Here, he admits to being 'in an almost sexless state, which is normal or at any rate common in boys of that age' (1970 [1952]: 402). Carefully, he teases out the chronology of his sexual awakening. At five or six 'like many children' (so aiming to generalise from the personal), he moves through a period of sexuality.

> My friends were the plumber's children up the road and we used sometimes to play games of a vaguely erotic kind. One was called 'playing at doctors' and I remember getting a faint but definitely pleasant thrill from holding a toy trumpet, which was supposed to be a stethoscope, against a little girl's belly (ibid: 403).

RICHARD LANCE KEEBLE

Next, he falls deeply in love with a girl named Elsie. And he goes on to dwell on his boyhood sexual confusions with what appears compelling honesty (though it may well be all fiction). Most of the Facts of Life (those capital letters indicating their Importance and Severity) are learned through watching animals. The section climaxes with him noticing his penis sometimes standing of its own accord – and his feeling shame (ibid).

NINETEEN EIGHTY-FOUR – AND THE JULIA CONUNDRUM

Sexual politics lie at the heart of *Nineteen Eighty-Four*. According to Cass R. Sunstein (2005: 241):

> Orwell suggests that totalitarian governments favour 'sexual puritanism', which induces 'hysteria', something that such governments mobilize in their own favour. This is the image of patriotic frenzy as 'sex gone sour'. On this view, sexual freedom embodies freedom and individualism, and it is the deepest enemy of a totalitarian state. A state that allows sexual freedom will be unable to repress its citizens.

Or, as Robin West stresses (2005: 248): 'Erotic sex. Winston Smith insists in *Nineteen Eighty-Four*, is a truly *political* and even revolutionary act.'

Yet, Orwell's representation of Julia, the woman who has a furtive affair with the anti-hero Winston Smith, has drawn particular wrath from feminist critics. For Patai, Orwell evokes yet another female stereotype in representing Julia as a rebel only 'from the waist downwards': she is motivated only by a love of sexual pleasure and is totally uninterested in the political dynamics of the society that oppresses her (Patai 1984: 243). When Winston reads to her from the book, supposedly written by the leader of the rebellion, Goldstein, she falls asleep (ibid: 244).

But what if Julia is actually a member of the Party, luring Winston Smith into a honeytrap? Gordon Bowker is one of the few critics to suspect Julia is actually not quite what she might appear:

> Julia seems to be a secret hater of the Party and Big Brother, seems to be a candidate for the dissident Brotherhood, seems to go off to be tortured after her arrest and finally seems to have been purged of her thought crime. But in the world of the book she could, like O'Brien [first friend of Smith and then torturer] and Charrington [owner of the junk shop who turns out to be working for the Party] also be a dissembler leading Winston straight into the arms of the Thought Police. On Airstrip One, truth rests on ever-shifting sands, only pain and Room 101 are real. Such a reading gives the book a strangely modern character making it a novel about the slippery unstable nature of meaning (2003: 388-389).

Orwell offers various clues: when Smith first sees her, she is arriving at the Two Minutes Hate session with, of all people, O'Brien (Orwell 2000 [1949]: 12). When he is later leaving Charrington's shop, he sees Julia:

> There was no doubting any longer that the girl was spying on him. She must have followed him here, because it was not credible that by pure chance she should have happened to be walking on the same evening up the same obscure backstreet, kilometres distant from any quarter where Party members lived. It was too great a co-incidence. Whether she was really an agent of the Thought Police, or simply an amateur spy activated by officiousness, hardly mattered. It was enough that she was watching him.

In the context of this interpretation, Julia's falling asleep whilst Winston reads from Goldstein's *The Theory and Practice of Oligarchical Collectivism* (the title a satirical jibe at all those tedious, theoretical left wing tracts that bored Orwell so much) is completely understandable (ibid: 247). As a Party spy she would find the book totally boring – and sleep-inducing. Moreover, seeing Julia as a spy can lead to two further contrasting interpretations. On the one hand it can be seen as subverting the conventional image of her: instead of being a submissive sex object she becomes a highly politicised agent of the state, influencing events in major ways. Or, as Tim Crook (2018) argues: 'There is still a valid feminist criticism of this dimension of the characterisation in deploying and demeaning the woman as a stereotypical Mata Hari-type honeytrap where women feature almost exclusively as the corrupting and seducing agents of sexpionage.'

ORWELL'S CHANGING ATTITUDES TOWARDS WOMEN

Orwell was a complex man, full of contradictions. Newsinger even detects a shift in his attitudes towards women during the Second World War (2018: 154). For instance, in August 1945, he wrote a sympathetic review of Virginia Woolf's *A Room of One's Own* in which she explores some of the reasons why women have not produced 'literature of the first order'. And he concludes with the comment that 'almost anyone of the male sex could read it with advantage' (ibid: 125).

Orwell's whole life can be considered an educational project. He had an enormous appetite and curiosity about life – a deep desire to understand himself and the times he was living in. And through his wonderfully original and often witty writings he was seeking to encourage us all to join him on his journey (Keeble 2016). As a result, he is constantly surprising us. For instance, in one of the 'As I Please' columns (28 July 1944) he wrote for the leftist weekly *Tribune* between 1943 and 1947, he even comments perceptively

RICHARD LANCE KEEBLE on the appeal of women's magazines such as *Lucky Star*, the *Golden Star*, *Peg's Paper*, *Secrets* and the *Oracle*. A woman has written to him pointing out that while stories in these mags often highlighted unemployment, in contrast, trade unions and socialism were never mentioned (Anderson 2006: 167). In response, Orwell suggests that such mags deal essentially in fantasies that sublimate the class struggle and aim to make a lot of money for the publishers. He continues:

> But, curiously enough, reality does enter into these women's magazines, not through the stories but through the correspondence columns, especially in those papers that give free medical advice. Here you can read harrowing tales of 'bad legs' and haemorrhoids written by middle-aged women who give themselves such pseudonyms as 'A Sufferer'. 'Mother of Nine' and 'Always Constipated'. To compare these letters with the love stories that lie cheek by jowl with them is to see how vast a part mere day-dreaming plays in modern life (ibid: 168).

In another column on 28 April 1944, he considers the right of women to wear make-up after a juvenile magistrate in London's East End has complained about girls of 14 dressing and talking like those of 18 and 19 and putting 'the same filth and muck on their faces' (ibid: 132). In reply, Orwell says that 'one of the big failures in human history has been the agelong attempt to stop women painting their faces'. Then, he even provides a potted history of women's make-up!

> The philosophers of the Roman empire denounced the frivolity of the modern woman in almost the same terms as she is denounced today. In the fifteenth century the church denounced the damnable habit of plucking the eyebrows. The English puritans, the Bolsheviks and the Nazis all attempted to discourage cosmetics, without success. In Victorian England rouge was considered so disgraceful that it was usually sold under some other name, but it continued to be used (ibid).

And on 8 November 1944, Orwell devoted the first section of his 'As I Please' column to examining in some considerable detail an American fashion magazine (ibid: 317). He takes care to list the content of the pictures: ball dresses, mink coats, step-ins, panties, brassieres, silk stockings, slippers, perfumes, lipsticks, nail varnish 'and, of course, women, unbelievably beautiful, who wear them or make use of them' (ibid). He next observes 'the striking prose style of the advertisements': 'an extraordinary mixture of sheer lushness with clipped and sometimes very expressive technical jargon'. And with a typically Orwellian flourish, he focuses on what's missing:

A fairly diligent search through the magazine reveals two discreet allusions to grey hair, but if there is anywhere a direct mention of fatness or middle age I have not found it. Birth and death are not mentioned either: not is work, except that a few recipes for breakfast dishes are given. The male sex enters directly or indirectly into perhaps one advertisement in twenty and photographs of dogs or kittens appear here and there. In only two pictures, out of about three hundred, is a child represented (ibid: 318).

Orwell is said to have virtually invented the discipline of cultural studies with his entirely original examinations of everyday things such as boys' weeklies, cups of tea, the common toad, trashy American crime novels, pubs, common lodging houses and handwriting (Keeble 2016). In addition, he commented on women's fashion magazines, make-up and journals such as *Lucky Star* and *Peg's Paper*. All this certainly reveals another side of Orwell's character that feminist critics have significantly ignored.

DRAWING CONCLUSIONS FROM MCGILL'S POSTCARDS

One of Orwell's most original studies of popular culture focused on the sexy seaside postcards of Donald McGill – published in Cyril Connolly's literary journal *Horizon* in September 1941.[3] According to John Sutherland, Orwell began collecting these postcards at about the age of twelve (2016: 77). 'They were available at newsagents in seaside Eastbourne (not Henley). Not all newsagents would let children buy them, but some would, particularly stands around the pier' (ibid; see also Crick 1980: 91). In her memoir, *Eric and Us* (2006 [1974]) Jacintha Buddicom remembers him showing her a selection of his 'less naughty McGill items' (ibid). Many considered the cartoons pornographic. In fact, some years after Orwell died, in May 1954, McGill was actually held in a police cell for an hour while awaiting trial over the allegedly obscene representation of a stick of rock – appearing in a cartoon like a giant penis. He was fined £50, had costs of £25 to pay plus his own, higher legal costs. While he had prepared a defence, he pleaded guilty on legal advice (Kennedy 2004; Barrell 2012).

These were, then, highly controversial cartoons 'with their endless succession of fat women in tight bathing dresses and their crude drawing and unbearable colours' (Orwell 1965 [1941]: 142). Biographer Colls describes them as 'dirty' and 'smutty-humorous' (2013: 155). Yet Orwell relishes in the sexuality of the images – and their humour.

The wording of the title of the essay is profoundly important. For Orwell deliberately subverts all traditional notions about cultural values – which rate the plays of Shakespeare and the novels of Jane Austen, say, as Art and sexy seaside postcards as non-Art. So the

RICHARD LANCE KEEBLE

title emphasises Orwell's central point – that McGill's cartoons were to be taken seriously as Art – with a capital 'A'. Irony is defined by John Sutherland as 'saying one thing and meaning another' (2011: 93) The etymological origin of the word – the Greek *eironeia* – translates as 'deception', 'hypocrisy' or 'lie'. In literature, irony makes simple things more slippery – but by doing so, truer to life. The title 'Such, Such Were the Joys' is ironic. But there is nothing ironic about 'The Art of Donald McGill.'

THE SUBTLE DEPLOYMENT OF *FAUX* SHAME

Orwell uses a number of subtle strategies to win over the somewhat highbrow readers of *Horizon* whom he presumes in the text will not be acquainted with the postcards (though many of the male readers may well have secretly acquired their own store – like Orwell…). He begins by providing an explanatory overview: 'They are a *genre* of their own, specializing in very "low" humour, the mother-in-law, baby's nappy, policemen's-boot type of joke and distinguishable from all the other kinds by having no artistic pretensions' (ibid, italics in the original). Next, he expresses *faux* shame:

> Your first impression is of overpowering vulgarity. This is quite apart from the ever-present obscenity and apart also from the hideousness of the colours. They have an utter lowness of mental atmosphere which comes not only in the nature of the jokes but, even more, in the grotesque, staring blatant quality of the drawings (ibid: 143).

But none of this outrage prevents Orwell from pressing on to analyse the content. First, he identifies the main subject areas: sex, home life, drunkenness, WC jokes, inter-working class snobbery and stock figures. He highlights both the visible and (equally interesting) the invisible (see Keeble 2015c: 18). 'Foreigners seldom ever appear. The chief locality joke is the Scotsman, who is almost inexhaustible. The lawyer is always a swindler, the clergyman always a nervous idiot who says the wrong thing' (op cit: 146). He also links the postcards' 'low' form of comedy with the music hall ribaldry of Max Miller. As Peter Marks stresses (2011: 123): 'Both the postcards and music hall, of course, primarily are working class forms of entertainment, expressing an earthy and open attitude to life's hardships.'

ENDORSING THE 'SANCHO PANZA VIEW OF LIFE'

Having set the scene, attempting to win over his readers with his *faux* shame and serious analysis, Orwell moves on to translate the real pleasure he derives from the sexy images and jokes into a profound discussion of the deeper social, class, moral and psychological aspects of the postcards. Their particular kind of humour only has meaning, he argues, in the context of a 'fairly strict moral code' (ibid: 148). And he reassures his highbrow readers that jokes about nagging wives and over-bearing mothers-in-law 'do at least imply a stable society in which marriage is indissoluble and family loyalty taken for granted' (ibid: 149). 'The postcards,' he suggests, 'give expression to the Sancho Panza view of life' – which Orwell goes on to endorse unreservedly.

> The Don Quixote-Sancho Panza combination ... is simply the ancient dualism of body and soul in fiction form ... Evidently, it corresponds to something enduring in our civilization, not in the sense that either character is to be found in a 'pure' state in real life, but in the sense that the two principles, noble folly and base wisdom, exist side by side in nearly every human being. If you look into your own mind, which are you, Don Quixote or Sancho Panza? Almost certainly you are both. There is one part of you that wishes to be a hero or a saint, but another part of you is a little fat man who seeks very clearly the advantages of staying alive with a white skin. He is your unofficial self, the voice of the belly protesting against the soul (ibid: 151-152).

For Crick (1980: 436), this amounts to nothing less than a profound comment about 'the uncrushable life-force of the common people' while Colls (2013: 156) suggests it reflects his 'devotion to a politics of actually existing ordinariness'.

Orwell's imagined audience is clearly male here – as he addresses his reader as 'he' and being 'unfaithful to your wife' (ibid: 152). But by now he is relishing in the raw sexuality of the cartoons – so his writing shifts to pronouncing (with tremendous *éclat*) on the complexities of the human condition and the social function of jokes. 'Codes of law and morals, or religious systems never have much room in them for the humorous view of life. Whatever is funny is subversive, every joke is ultimately a custard pie' (ibid). Is Orwell right here? In stressing the subversive role of humour, he is revelling in being the dissident, the controversialist, the maverick. But not all jokes play this role. For instance, the wit and mockery of the court jester in the Middle Ages essentially served the interests of the court, while today sexist, racist, ageist jokes merely reinforce dominant prejudices (Keeble 2015c: 18-19).

Orwell ends the essay in a droll, witty, aphoristic sort of way: 'On the whole, human beings want to be good, but not too good, and not quite all the time' (ibid: 154).

CONCLUSION

Orwell's representations of gender have long interested academics. His treatment of sexuality, in contrast, has been little covered by Orwellian commentators. Yet this paper has argued that sex lies at the core of much of Orwell's writings. The gloomy, dystopian vision of *Nineteen Eighty-Four*, his most celebrated novel, has probably helped create a public image of Orwell as a gloomy, pessimistic, humourless and – in the context of this paper – a rather unsexual man.[4] In fact, the opposite is the case. For his times, Orwell was remarkably open about sexual matters, even his homoerotic tendencies – and the development of his own sexuality. In *Down and Out in Paris and London* and the essay 'Such, Such were the Joys' he confronted issues around homosexuality quite bravely – since it was then illegal and gays faced awful discrimination.

Feminist critics are right to point to the largely negative representations of women in his writings. But this paper has highlighted writings – often ignored – that reveal a very different side to Orwell: happy to deconstruct in detail a women's fashion magazine or outline, in brief, the history of women's make-up. The suggestion here that Julia, Winston Smith's lover in *Nineteen Eighty-Four*, is a possible Party spy luring the rebel Winston into a honeytrap aims to challenge conventional interpretations. Moreover, Orwell's *Horizon* essay on Donald McGill's postcards amounts to a joyful affirmation of the hedonistic, Sancho Panza attitude to life - and a celebration, nothing less, of the pleasures of sex.

NOTES

[1] See also Levy, Paul (2016) How does the last surviving member of the Bloomsbury set celebrate her 100th birthday? *Guardian*, 17 June. Available online at https://www.telegraph.co.uk/women/life/how-does-the-last-surviving-member-of-the-bloomsbury-set-celebra/, accessed on 13 August 2018

[2] See https://www.orwellfoundation.com/the-orwell-foundation/orwell/poetry/the-italian-soldier-shook-my-hand/

[3] A Donald McGill Museum has opened in Ryde, Isle of White. See https://saucyseasidepostcards.com/

[4] For instance, biographer Jeffrey Meyers (2000: 376-377), in his index, lists 37 characteristics (from 'attitude to animals', 'austerity' and 'cockiness' to 'violent temper' and 'working class persona'). But there is no mention of sexuality. Similarly, biographer D. J. Taylor (2003:) also has 37 entries under 'Attitudes, habits and characteristics' in his Index (from 'Animals, love of' to 'Working classes, attitude to') but there is no mention of sex or sexuality. Bernard Crick (1980: 653-654) lists 'sadism, accusations of GO's', 'self-pity', 'smoking habits' and 'sterility' but there is no category for 'sexuality'. In contrast, Gordon Bowker (my favourite biographer) has 25 entries under 'sex and sexuality' in his Index (2003: 491)

REFERENCES

Anderson, Paul (ed.) (2006) *Orwell in Tribune: 'As I Please' and Other Writings 1943-7*, London: Politico's

Barrell, Tony (2012) May the sauce be with you, *Sunday Times Magazine*, 20 February pp 52-55

Beddoe, Deirdre (1984) Hindrances and help-meets: Women in the writings of George Orwell, Norris, Christopher (ed.) *Inside the Myth: Orwell: Views from the Left*, London: Lawrence and Wishart pp 139-154

Bluemel, Kristin (2012) The intimate Orwell: Women's production, feminist consumption, Keeble, Richard Lance (ed.) *Orwell Today*, Bury St Edmunds: Abramis pp 15-29

Bowker, Gordon (2003) *George Orwell*, London: Little, Brown

Brennan, Michael G. (2017) *George Orwell and Religion*, London and New York: Bloomsbury

Buddicom, Jacintha (2006 [1974]) *Eric and US: A Remembrance of George Orwell*, UK: Finlay Publishers, revised edition edited by Venables, Dione

Campbell, Beatrix (1984) Orwell: Paterfamilias or Big Brother?, Norris, Christopher (ed.) *Inside the Myth: Orwell: Views from the Left*, London: Lawrence and Wishart pp 128-136

Colls, Robert (2013) *George Orwell: English Rebel*, Oxford: Oxford University Press

Crick, Bernard (1980) *George Orwell: A Life*, Harmondsworth, Middlesex: Penguin

Crook, Tim (2018) On Julia and sexpionage, in an email to the author, 20 September 2018

Davison, Peter (ed.) (2010) *George Orwell: A Life in Letters*, London and New York: Penguin

Keeble, Richard Lance (2015a) Homage to literary journalism, *orwellsocietyblog*, 24 November. Available online at https://orwellsoc1ietyblog.wordpress.com/2015/11/24/homage-to-literary-journalism-in-homage/, accessed on 15 August 2018

Keeble, Richard Lance (2015b) Orwell and the war reporter's imagination, Keeble, Richard Lance (ed.) *George Orwell Now!*, New York: Peter Lang pp 209-224

Keeble, Richard Lance (2015c) 'There is always room for one more custard pie': Orwell's humour, Keeble, Richard Lance and Swick, David (eds) *Pleasures of the Prose: Journalism and Humour*, Bury St Edmunds: Abramis pp 10-25

Keeble, Richard Lance (2016) Orwell, the university and the university of life. Keynote talk at Orwell symposium, Goldsmiths, University of London, 10 January. Available online at https://orwellsocietyblog.wordpress.com/2016/01/10/orwell-the-university-and-the-university-of-life/

Keeble, Richard Lance (2018) 'Such, Such Were the Joys' and the journalistic imagination, *George Orwell Studies*, Vol. 2, No. 2 pp 69-90

Kennedy, Maev (2004) Exhibition marks 50 years of holding back the sauce, *Guardian*, 22 May

Koven, Seth (2006) *Slumming: Sexual and Social Politics in Victorian London*, Princeton and Oxford: Princeton University Press

Marks, Peter (2011) *George Orwell the Essayist: Literature, Politics and the Periodical Culture*, London and New York: Continuum

Meyers, Jeffrey (2000) *Orwell: Wintry Conscience of a Generation*, New York and London: W. W. Norton and Company Ltd

Newsinger, John (2018) *Hope Lies in the Proles: George Orwell and the Left*, London: Pluto Press

Orwell, George (1980 [1933]) *Down and Out in Paris and London, George Orwell: Complete and Unabridged*, London: Secker and Warburg/Octopus pp 15-120

Orwell, George (1962 [1941]) The Art of Donald McGill, *Decline of the English Murder and Other Essays*, Harmondsworth, Middlesex: Penguin pp 142-154

RICHARD LANCE KEEBLE

Orwell, George (1970 [1952]) Such, Such Were the Joys, Orwell, Sonia and Angus, Ian (eds) *The Collected Essays, Journalism and Letters, Vol. 4: In Front of Your Nose 1945-1950*, Harmondsworth, Middlesex: Penguin Books pp 379-422

Orwell, George (2000 [1949]) *Nineteen Eighty-Four*, London: Penguin Classics

Orwell, Sonia and Angus, Ian (eds) (1970) *The Collected Essays, Journalism and Letters of George Orwell, Vol. 1: An Age Like This*, Harmondsworth: Middlesex

Patai, Daphne (1984) *The Orwell Mystique: A Study in Male Ideology*, Amherst: University of Massachusetts Press

Seshagiri, Urmila (2001) Misogyny and anti-imperialism in George Orwell's *Burmese Days*, Lázaro, Alberto (ed.) *The Road from George Orwell*, Bern: Peter Lang pp 105-119

Sunstein, Cass R. (2005) Sexual freedom and political freedom, Gleason, Abbott, Goldsmith, Jack and Nussbaum, Martha C. (eds) *On Nineteen Eighty-Four: Orwell and Our Future*, Princeton: Princeton University Press pp 233-241

Sutherland, John (2011) *50 Literature Ideas You Really Need to Know*, London: Quercus

Sutherland, John (2016) *Orwell's Nose: A Pathological Biography*, London: Reaktion Books

Taylor, D. J. (2003) *Orwell: The Life*, London: Chatto and Windus

West, Robin (2005) Sex, law, power and community, Gleason, Abbott, Goldsmith, Jack and Nussbaum, Martha C. (eds) *On Nineteen Eighty-Four: Orwell and Our Future*, Princeton: Princeton University Press pp 242-260

Williams, Kristian (2017) *Between the Bullet and the Lie: Essays on Orwell*, Chico, Oakland, Edinburgh, Baltimore: AK Press

NOTE ON THE CONTRIBUTOR

Richard Lance Keeble is chair of The Orwell Society, editor of *George Orwell Studies* and *Ethical Space: The International Journal of Communication Ethics*, Professor of Journalism at the University of Lincoln and Visiting Professor at Liverpool Hope University. He has written and edited 39 books on a range of media-related issues.

PAPER

Performance and Spectation in Orwell's *Burmese Days*

DOUGLAS KERR

It is productive to think of empire, and Orientalism, as a series of performative encounters. Orwell anticipated this theatrical vision in a narrative such as 'Shooting an Elephant'. This paper centres on an episode in Burmese Days *in which Flory, the central character, takes the newly-arrived Elizabeth Lackersteen to see a Burmese* pwe *dance, performed in a street in the town of Kyauktada. The English visitors are both spectators of the performance and the crowd and the objects of curious spectation by the local audience. The episode offers a complex analysis of the dynamics of performance, spectation and interpretation, with Flory and Elizabeth bringing to bear quite different anthropological attitudes (to the Burmese) and aesthetic expectations (of the show, which their own intrusion also modifies). The* pwe *itself bears an interesting relation to both highbrow and popular Western ideas of performance – and of the Orient – in the period of modernism, from* The Rite of Spring *to* Chu Chin Chow.

Keywords: Orwell, performance, spectation, *Burmese Days*

CHU CHIN CHOW: ORIENT AND UTOPIA

Orwell excelled in several literary genres but it's fair to say he is not best known for his theatre criticism. Some of this work dates from perhaps the most demoralising year of his life, 1940, when he was desperate to make some contribution to the war effort but found himself with nothing better to do than what he considered trivial and humiliating hack work.[1] As the early engagements of the Battle of Britain were staged in the skies above southern England, Orwell was in the stalls of the Palace Theatre, London, with his notebook, watching a performance of *Chu Chin Chow*, a popular musical based on the story of Ali Baba. He was reviewing it for *Time and Tide*.[2] 'I do not think I was the only person in the audience who wondered to himself, "Is it really possible that this tripe once ran for five years continuously? And if so, why?"' (*CWGO* 12: 215). *Chu Chin Chow* had first been performed in London in 1916, in the depths of the Great War, and had proved extraordinarily popular with soldiers on leave from the front.

DOUGLAS KERR

You came back with the mud of Flanders still on your boots, plunged into a Turkish bath, then went to dinner at the Criterion and then went to *Chu Chin Chow*. The charm lay in the fantastic unreality of the whole thing, and the droves of women, practically naked and painted to an agreeable walnut-juice tint. It was a never-never land, the 'gorgeous East', where, as is well known, everyone has fifty wives and spends his time lying on a divan, eating pomegranates. In this vulgar spectacle a doomed generation of boys got a sort of dreamlike glimpse of all the ease and pleasure that they would never have (ibid: 216-217).

The production may have been 'tripe', but Orwell is far from despising the state of mind in which its original audience enjoyed it. Why did these doomed boys flock to see *Chu Chin Chow*, despite its 'fantastic unreality'? It confirmed a kind of knowledge about the East ('where, as is well known, everyone has fifty wives' and so on) which nowadays we would call Orientalism in the sense the word was given by Edward W. Said in the book of that name (Said 1978). At the same time it presented a spectacle of the Orient as a kind of utopia, a 'dreamlike glimpse' of a desirable ease and pleasure extremely removed from what awaited these soldiers when they returned to duty in France or Flanders. Watching this gaudy confection in the midst of the Second World War, Orwell sees the performance as Orientalist, and the spectation (the act of witnessing and interpretation) as utopian. Orient and utopia provide me with two important terms for the discussion that follows. The review is also helpful as a reminder, from Orwell, that any theatrical production is a transaction between performers and audience, and that what happens on the stage is only half the story.

EMPIRE AND PERFORMANCE

Writers as differently oriented as David Cannadine (2001) and Homi Bhabha (1985) have found it useful to think of empire itself in terms of a series of performative encounters. Bhabha productively pays attention to the staging of conversations between rulers and ruled. Cannadine shows how the British understood the need to perform their power with a gaudy reproduction of their way of life before their subject peoples: in performing that power, they brought it into being. Their imperial rule depended on armed force or the threat of it, but it rested even more on hegemony, the consent of the ruled, manufactured by the spectacle of the confidence of the rulers, their power, splendour, and what appeared to be a natural authority. In this sense empire was performance, an example of 'show business'.

It is not very productive to question the authenticity of such demonstrations – to what extent did the extraordinary pomp of the Delhi Durbar of 1911 give an accurate picture of the British? – and it would be rash to assume that all the performers played their parts well, willingly or knowingly in the show. Meanwhile, at the same time as observing these spectacles of authority and legitimacy, the subject peoples were themselves the objects of spectation, as foreign administrators, scholars, policemen and tourists sought to interpret their appearance and speech and behaviour, in all its seductive or horrifying difference, and convert that interpretation into knowledge. The atomic structure of empire is made of a huge network of performances, from the Delhi Durbar to the songs sung by his ayah to the infant Rudyard Kipling. The essential constituents of performance are performer and audience, yet there is also always a thoroughly dialogic reciprocity. The audience modify the performance, and are themselves the objects of spectation by the performers and each other.

Orwell's novel *Burmese Days* (*BD*) (1989a [1934]) is full of such performances and spectations; indeed, it can be said to be structured around them, and in a moment I will focus on one episode in the book, the *pwe* dance attended by John Flory and Elizabeth Lackersteen in Chapter 8. This is a case of an actual theatrical production in which there is a quite complex analysis of the criss-cross dynamics of performance and spectation, and of ethnographic and aesthetic spectacle and interpretation, onstage and in the audience. First though, the story 'Shooting an Elephant' (1936) can provide an illustration of Orwell's understanding of what we might call the performativity of empire.

It is a highly dramatic, theatrical story. The officer who narrates it begins by remembering the hatred with which he was viewed by large numbers of the restive population of Burma, under whose hostile gaze, he feels, he was always on show. (The story is full of the vocabulary of looking and seeing.) When word reaches him of a rogue elephant which has killed a man, and he makes his way to the scene, he realises he has attracted a crowd of hundreds of local people. This mobile audience follows him with clear expectations, and his next realisation is that this means he is not free to choose whether or not to shoot the animal. With the rifle in his hands, he has been cast as a figure of imperial authority, 'seemingly', as he says, 'the leading actor of the piece' (*CWGO* 10: 504).[3] Though his instincts and his reason tell him it is not necessary to shoot the now docile beast, there is a script at work here that dictates that this is absolutely what he must do. He has to give the public what they want, which is a kind of ritual, a performance of a violent domination of nature in the style of Rider Haggard's white hunter Allan Quatermain (1887). The show must go on.

In this imperial drama, the British officer feels he has less agency than the audience of colonised people who despise him, and so he proceeds with an act of extreme bad faith and shoots the animal. 'A sahib has got to act like a sahib,' in both senses, and he realises that 'when the white man turns tyrant it is his own freedom that he destroys' (*CWGO* 10: 504). This famous insight is, of course, itself less than half the story because, though the Burmese crowd call the shots, they have even less freedom to act in this horrible drama. In colonised Burma, the population were forbidden by law to carry firearms (Maung Htin Aung 1967: 280), and there is nothing the locals can do in this crisis except to watch the white man act.

BURMESE DAYS: EMPIRE AS SHOW BUSINESS

It happens that the drama of the elephant shooting is anticipated more than once in *Burmese Days* in the form of a structural homology. In the novel, Flory first meets Elizabeth when he hears a cry for help, and finds the English girl cowering against a bush, apparently menaced by a large water-buffalo (*BD*: 80-82). Flory is able to deal with this by going up to the animal and smacking it on the nose, whereupon it timidly lumbers away. Flory knows that water buffalo are domesticated farm animals, slow-witted and harmless, but Elizabeth insists on believing that this opportune white hero has courageously rescued her from a murderous Oriental beast. In other words, because of her paranoid expectations of what Burma is like (which are ideological in origin), she reads Flory's mundane action as epic theatre, and him as a dashing hero of imperial romance.

In order to continue to impress her, Flory has to reproduce this successful performance of white authority over the environment. Later when he takes Elizabeth on an outing into the jungle (ibid: 162-180), he feels the need to play the role of white hunter, blasting away at the wildlife which earlier we have seen him communing with like a Wordsworthian (ibid: 55-60). It is show business again, and Flory is showing off to Elizabeth with a performance of the kind of English manhood she has been educated or miseducated to admire and expect. But again, he is miscast, caught in what we can call bad performance, for in earlier scenes of his solitary visits to the jungle we have been shown that Flory is better suited by temperament to wield a butterfly net than an elephant gun. But performativity, again in the form of the ideologically-constructed expectations of his audience, has taken away his freedom.

He can't play the Wordsworthian nature lover, he must play the white hunter. As for the platform on which these dramas are played out, the natural environment of colonised Burma, we are dealing here with two rival Western utopias of the East, each with a long tradition in European Orientalism. One is of the Orient as a stage for the performance of white masculine domination, the imperial romance adventure. The other envisages the Orient as a fecund pastoral, a paradise of exotic if fragile nature. One utopia points to the Imperial War Museum, the other to Kew Gardens.

THE *PWE* DANCE: PERFORMANCE AND SPECTATION

And so we come to the *pwe* dance. This happens in the early stages of Flory's and Elizabeth's relationship; in fact, it is their first date. (He has shaved, and instructed his servant to lay out his best Palm Beach suit.) He takes her for a walk in the town one evening and they come upon a *pwe* dance in the street, paid for and presided over by the wily villain U Po Kyin, the sub-divisional magistrate who will later accomplish Flory's downfall. Anxious to show off Burma to this newcomer from Europe, Flory invites Elizabeth to sit and watch the show, and a complex of performativity unfolds in the dusty Burmese street.

The *pwe* is a dramatic entertainment inseparable from the many Burmese religious festivals. It is typically performed on a makeshift platform erected in the street, and offers a mixture of dance, pantomime, slapstick and religious drama. We have a valuable account of how the *pwe* looked to an outsider in Norman Lewis's *Golden Earth*, published in 1952 within twenty years of *Burmese Days*; it is quite similar to the production described in Orwell's novel (Lewis 1952: 27-34). In fact, what Flory and Elizabeth witness is a sort of warm-up act, the performance of clowns and a female dancer which, though several hours in duration, is the prelude to straight theatrical shows which go on till dawn. Lewis, like Flory, is fascinated by the dancer.

> She was a tiny, doll-like creature with a face that was plain and sullen even in repose. But as soon as she began to dance she became transfigured. She had all the poise and fire of a Spanish flamenco dancer, plus the snake-like head and eye movements of an Indian. To this she added the Burmese speciality of thrusting out her arms in such extraordinary positions that they appeared to be dislocated at the elbows. … Sometimes the clowns joined in, dancing in mimicry of the actress who, as soon as she had finished her piece, would suddenly relapse into a set pose, turn her back on the public, and squatting on her heels, make up her face or drink tea (ibid: 28-29).

The *pwe* is a traditional entertainment put on for the enjoyment of a local audience. It is not addressed to the European visitors, but this one is modified for their benefit: when they arrive, U Po Kyin arranges for the programme to be changed so that they can witness the star dancer, out of her proper sequence in the programme. As this is a literary essay and not an anthropological one, I will concentrate on the reactions and interpretations of Flory and Elizabeth, rather than the local audience. But as we have seen before, the drama of performance and spectation is multi-directional. Flory and Elizabeth react (differently) to the Burmese audience as well as to the performers, and the locals observe the Europeans as well as their compatriots onstage.

DOUGLAS KERR

The blonde Elizabeth, indeed, has been an object of fascination since her recent arrival in Kyauktada, ogled lasciviously by the men in the European club, and observed with perhaps more innocent interest by the Burmese. On her first visit to Flory's house, she is alarmed to find an *ad hoc* audience of some dozen locals has gathered to have a look at her, gazing at this exotic creature, 'as English yokels might gaze at a Zulu warrior in full regalia' (*BD*: 88). This is an ethnographic but also a performative moment – for these spectators, Elizabeth is performing English womanhood, just as surely as Flory will later perform English manhood for her in the Burmese jungle. A moment later, Orwell's Burmese mistress Ma Hla May makes an embarrassing appearance and the two women stare at each other uncomprehendingly. 'For the best part of a minute neither of them could take her eyes from the other; but which found the spectacle more grotesque, more incredible, there is no saying.' 'Oh, is *that* what Burmese women are like?' says Elizabeth (ibid: 89).[4]

Now at the *pwe* dance, Elizabeth is covertly scrutinised by those around her even as she and Flory concentrate on the onstage spectacle, which – as in the double spectation with Ma Hla May on Flory's verandah – presents a contrasting show of womanhood. The *pwe* dancer, her face covered in white powder, goes through her grotesque, inorganic-looking postures, 'precisely like a jointed doll, and yet incredibly sinuous' (ibid: 106). The dance approaches a climax.

> With that dead-white oval face and those wooden gestures she was monstrous, like a demon. ... Still in that strange bent posture the girl turned round and danced with her buttocks protruded towards the audience. Her silk *longyi* gleamed like metal. With hands and elbows still rotating she wagged her posterior from side to side. Then – astonishing feat, quite visible through the *longyi* – she began to wriggle her two buttocks independently in time with the music.
>
> There was a shout of applause from the audience (ibid: 108-109).

Flory and Elizabeth respond differently to this remarkable performance. Flory has lived for years in Burma. Though weak and self-hating, he is a man of goodwill. He dislikes his thoroughly philistine European compatriots, whose idea of culture is 'whisky and Edgar Wallace' (ibid: 86), but he likes Burma and the Burmese. Now he has concluded that the new arrival is a kindred spirit and he is keen to help her to share his enthusiasm. 'You've read books and been in civilised places,' he tells Elizabeth, 'you're not like the rest of us miserable savages here. Don't you think this is worth watching, in its queer way?' (ibid: 107) For her benefit he keeps up a running commentary on the dancer's performance. It's grotesque, ugly, even sinister, he concedes. 'And yet when you look closely, what art, what centuries of culture you can see behind it!' He warms to his theme:

> In some way that I can't define to you, the whole life and spirit of Burma is summed up in the way that girl twists her arms. When you see her you can see the rice-fields, the villages under the teak trees, the pagodas, the priests in their yellow robes, the buffaloes swimming the rivers in the early morning, Thibaw's palace (ibid: 107-108).

Flory stops at this point, realising that 'he had only been talking like a character in a novel, and not a very good novel' (ibid: 108). Indeed, he is offering the body of the dancer to Elizabeth as both a tourist attraction (a 'sight' for the sightseer) and a living archive of knowledge about Burma. He is engaged in what Edward Said called 'radical typing', assuming an individual phenomenon must be somehow representative of the Orient as a whole (Said 1978: 231). Flory has overcome his aversion from the grotesque difference of the sight, and now applauds it as authentic, exotic and immemorial. And with his catalogue of sightseeing clichés – the rice-fields, the pagodas, and so on – he has conjured a soft-focus Orient which is just as much a utopia as the more vulgar one offered to the audience of *Chu Chin Chow*. The Burmese audience, partaking in a religious festival, responding to the ribaldry of the clowns, appreciating the skill of the dancer, and joining in the songs, are unlikely to see the performance in the same way.

Elizabeth, too, is inclined to see the dancer as typical of Burma, but for her this is no recommendation. Flory was wrong about her. Far from inculcating in her an appreciation for the arts, her two years in Paris with her slatternly mother have left her with a horror of anything artistic or intellectual, which she has come to associate with boring and incomprehensible conversation and bohemian squalor. She sees 'this nonsense of writing books and footling with paint brushes' (*BD*: 96) as the opposite of respectable and, besides, it seems to be associated with poverty. She is horrified now to find herself obliged to watch an apparently obscene dance, surrounded by a 'smelly native crowd' (ibid: 105). 'What was she doing in this place? Surely it was not right to be sitting among the black people like this, almost touching them, in the scent of their garlic and their sweat?'[5] (ibid: 108) This is paranoid Orientalism, the East as nightmare, embodied in a dance that seems unnatural, inhuman, and climaxes in a lewd gesture – the buttock-wriggling – that looks deliberately insulting. The show seems particularly provocative to her as a woman. When she met Ma Hla May, Elizabeth was not sure whether this was a man or a woman (ibid: 89). Now the androgynous-looking *pwe* dancer confronts her with a spectacle of womanhood not just alien but aggressively and jeeringly different from her own ladylike respectability.[6] Scandalised, she gets up and leaves, a disrespectful act that annoys the local audience.

The scandal is both ethnographic and aesthetic. To Elizabeth, the Burmese are 'people with black faces, almost savages' (ibid: 121). She thinks their appearance and their culture are ugly and primitive. Flory wants to educate her. He wishes she would not spectate Burma 'with the dull, incurious eyes of a memsahib'[7] (ibid 121). He imagines she must have spent her time in Paris sitting in 'cafés with foreign art students, drinking white wine and talking about Marcel Proust' (ibid: 86). But, in fact, her time there has done nothing to broaden her mind. In Paris, her idea of cultural utopia was to go to the American embassy and stare at society photographs in magazines from Britain like the *Sketch*, the *Tatler* and the *Sporting and Dramatic* – 'Lovely, lovely, golden world!' (ibid: 95-96). She remains insular, snobbish and philistine. In Kyauktada, she shrinks from both Burma and art: in Flory's bumbling interpretation of the *pwe* dance 'she had caught the hated word Art more than once' (ibid: 108).

Flory's spectation is much more sympathetic both to the Burmese and to the *pwe*. He is necessarily an ethnographic outsider, but he tries to make the imaginative effort to enter into the spirit of what he is seeing, alien though it is to him. There is some similarity here with what Orwell says in *Homage to Catalonia* about his own reaction as a foreigner in Barcelona at the beginning of 1937; what he saw there, he remembered, was 'queer and moving', although 'there was much in it that I did not understand, in some ways I did not even like it' (Orwell 1989b [1938]: 3). However, the most striking parallel for the performance criticism he whispers in Elizabeth's ear at the *pwe* is to be found in *Nineteen Eighty-Four* (1949), in the comments of Winston Smith to Julia, as they listen to the song of the prole woman outside the window of their love-nest. Here is another ugly-beautiful folk performance which the bourgeois observer sentimentalises and idealises as a utopia (Orwell 1989c [1949]: 227-229).[8] These echoes from elsewhere help to bring out the politics of performativity in *Burmese Days*. In Flory's and Elizabeth's spectation of the *pwe*, we can see two kinds of Orientalism, appreciative and denigratory, underlying two theories of empire, one liberal and sentimental, the other authoritarian and racist. (Neither, needless to say, can be imputed to George Orwell.)

THE *PWE*, MODERNISM AND PRIMITIVISM

Elizabeth is scandalised at the *pwe* dance, and she walks out. In her failure to respond warmly to this display of indigenous culture, she is playing the insular and intolerant memsahib of twentieth-century colonial fiction such as Forster's *A Passage to India* (1979 [1924]).[9] I want now to argue that at the same time she is being satirised in another, less obvious role. To make this argument, it is necessary to pivot on this word scandal, and to change the frame from the imperial critique of *Burmese Days* to the, perhaps, unexpected theme of Orwell and the modern performance arts. These arts often not only provoked scandal, but sought it out and wore it as a battle honour. The scandalised bourgeois (or bourgeoise) is a stock figure from the mythology of the modern European and American arts, especially the arts of modernism, and above all the avant-garde: in fact, it sometimes seems it was the scandal they provoked, from Duchamp to Dada, that authenticated them as modern.

Since the time of Baudelaire, the more modern and progressive of artists have accepted cheerfully the mission to *épater la bourgeoisie*, a motto especially associated with the city of Paris where, for example, Alfred Jarry's *Ubu Roi* (1896), Claude Debussy's *L'Après-Midi d'un Faune* (1894) and Igor Stravinsky's *Le Sacre du Printemps* (1913) performed by the Ballets Russes, and the dance of the Americans, Loïe Fuller, (1862-1928) and Isadora Duncan (1877-1927) were all brought before the public. These innovative performances were greeted with indignation and disgust by the more conservative elements of the theatre-going public. They were scandalous. They were disrespectful, iconoclastic if not obscene, and used an idiom of expression which was foreign and barbarous. Susan Jones writes of modernism's 'recovery and aestheticization of the atavistic' (Jones 2013: 110). As W. B. Yeats famously reflected after seeing the first public performance of *Ubu Roi* and its riotous reception in a Paris theatre in 1896: 'After us the Savage God' (Yeats 1955 [1914]: 348-349).[10]

The savagery was not just a figure of speech. All of the revolutionary productions mentioned above took some inspiration from what was referred to, in the idiom of the day, as the primitive. As the classics to the Renaissance, so was the primitive to modernism, whether in the form of Nietzsche's uncovering of the atavistic roots of European drama in *The Birth of Tragedy* (1872), the African masks in Picasso's *Les Demoiselles d'Avignon* (1907) or the fertility rituals coded into T. S. Eliot's *The Waste Land* (1922). The primitive might be found in folk art, like the crude rhythms and violent rituals that fuse Orientalism and Russian folklore, which are transformed in Stravinsky and Nijinsky's *Le Sacre du Printemps*. But inspiration was also sought from further afield, from the so-called primitive cultures of Africa and Asia, and making these cultures available to Western scholars and artists was one of the more interesting byproducts of imperialism.[11]

Modernist performance was typically shocking in content – it was unrestrained, for example, by bourgeois ideas of what was acceptable in terms of bodily functions and sexuality – and in form, in its willingness to experiment with a vocabulary of sound and movement that was no longer expressive, organic, fluent, individualistic, humanist and decorous in the manner of most performance art of the earlier nineteenth century. Modernist and avant-garde art liked to 'derealise' and 'deindividualise' its performers by masking them (or better still, making them actual marionettes),[12] to put them through movements that seemed unnatural and grotesque, to break up its own rhythms into fragments, to violate in every way the conventions of realistic representation and the theatre of illusion, and to defamiliarise its own language so as to create the deliberate effect of the foreign.[13] This violence done to traditional forms and manners was accompanied, by way of collateral damage, by the scandalising of the bourgeois. A deliberate aesthetic of shock defined itself against the tastes, expectations and morals of the conservative middle-class consumers of more traditional art.[14]

Flory likes the *pwe*, but even he describes it as queer, grotesque, ugly, sinister and diabolical (*BD*: 107). Elizabeth, who is already disposed to loathe it because it's Art, finds it 'a hideous and savage spectacle' (ibid: 110). An example of traditional Burmese folk art, it would, indeed, be considered primitive if measured against the middle-class theatre of the Parisian boulevards or London's West End. Arguably though, another way to put this would be to describe it as a modernist performance.[15]

Far from being framed in a plush theatre with a decorated proscenium and a 'fourth wall', the *pwe* takes place in open popular lived space, attracts all classes, and is actual street theatre. It does not mask its devices, like naturalistic drama. The dancer is dressed in ancient Burmese costume, but is first observed in plain sight squatting at the back of the stage, smoking a cigar, before she comes forward to perform; this is an alienation effect that might have been applauded by Bertholt Brecht.[16] Her thickly powdered face expresses neither 'character' (in the fictional or dramatic sense) nor emotion, nor even humanity – 'With that dead-white oval face and those wooden gestures she was monstrous, like a demon' (ibid: 108). The music, with bagpipes and plenty of percussion, is first described as a loud squalling, and later adopts 'a swift trochaic rhythm, gay yet fierce,' taken up by the crowd 'chanting the harsh syllables in unison' (ibid).[17] The dance itself is 'like the movements of one of those jointed wooden figures on an old-fashioned roundabout' (ibid: 106), and the doll-like *pwe* girl strikes grotesque and painful-looking postures – 'as though sitting down, knees bent, body leaned forward, with her arms extended and writhing' (ibid: 107) – a body language which would also impress Norman Lewis, who writes of 'the Burmese speciality of thrusting out her arms in such extraordinary positions that they appeared to be dislocated at the elbows' (Lewis 1952: 29). This emulation of the posture of a puppet might strike a Western observer – one acquainted perhaps with the theories of Edward Gordon Craig (see note 12) – as a 'realization of anti-realist and anti-romantic forms of dance' (Jones 2013: 216).[18] It was very modern, or, to put it differently, very primitive.[19]

Besides being itself an authentic Eastern folk tradition, the *pwe*, then, seems to contain much of the vocabulary of Western modern or modernist performing arts, in theatre, opera, and dance, and is consistent with the theory behind them. These techniques had evolved above all in the city of Paris, where the fictional Elizabeth Lackersteen lived for a miserable year in a squalid studio in Montparnasse, and where, in the years of 1928 and 1929, an actual young man named Eric Blair was living *la vie de Bohème* as a struggling literary expatriate, and incubating his first novel, *Burmese Days* (Taylor 2003: 93-102).[20] Elizabeth may have recoiled from the artistic world, but Blair – whose relation to the cultures of European modernism is under-researched – could hardly have been unaware of ongoing experiments in the performing arts in the city.[21]

It is not possible to establish whether Orwell consciously drew a line between the *pwe* and modernist performance, or whether the analogy is registered at the level of the unconscious of the text – in other words, whether the interpretation of the *pwe* as analogous to modernism was part of Orwell's deliberate intention, or arises *ex post facto* from a non-authorial reading of the text.[22] The resemblances are there, and they give an extra dimension to Elizabeth Lackersteen's revulsion from the *pwe*, putting it in the tradition of the theatrical *scandales* that are an important part of the history of the modern theatre, and casting her in the role of the outraged philistine.

From *Ubu Roi* to John Millington Synge's *The Playboy of the Western World* (1907), from *L'Après-Midi d'un Faune* to Samuel Beckett's *Waiting for Godot* (1953), there has always been a troop of scandalised bourgeois ready to interrupt the action or flounce out of the theatre in protest. Elizabeth has watched the *pwe* with the classic symptoms of 'a mixture of amazement, boredom and something approaching horror' (*BD*: 107). Flory's Orientalist utopia is to her a spectacle of ugliness and insult, the Orient as abjection. The last straw is the buttock-wiggling of the dancer. Are the buttocks a scatological or an erotic sign? No matter. For Elizabeth, they are too much, and she gets up and leaves. In this public rejection – 'making a scene' – she is unwittingly playing one final role. As the narrow-minded, body-denying, philistine, respectable, ridiculous, spectating bourgeois, she is giving an excellent if unintended performance of the essential fool of modernism.

DOUGLAS KERR

NOTES

[1] 'The incongruity of having to pursue the mundane tasks of reviewing at a time when there seemed every chance that the country would shortly be invaded was not lost on the literary journalists of 1940.' Taylor (2003: 283)

[2] Orwell's review was published in *Time and Tide* on 13 July 1940 (*CWGO* 12: 215-216)

[3] In the previous sentence he says he is watched like 'a conjurer about to perform a trick', which gives a further idea of the kind of production he is in

[4] Ma Hla May's greatest performance will come in the *coup de théâtre* at the climax of the novel (*BD* : 284-286), staged in the European church, where she plays the role of Wronged Woman, ably coached by U Po Kyin, and brings about Flory's disgrace

[5] See the chapter on Oriental crowds in Kerr (2008: 53-78)

[6] However, though not given to suggestive buttock-wiggling, Elizabeth is as much on display in Kyauktada as the *pwe* girl. Obliged by straitened circumstances to commodify herself, she has come to Burma to attract an English husband. Meeting the apparently eligible bachelor Verrall for the first time, she quickly makes an impression on him by 'dancing very close together, her body bent backwards under his' (ibid. 217)

[7] The influence of E. M. Forster's *A Passage to India* (1979 [1924]) is particularly strong in Orwell's treatment of this theme of English ways of 'seeing' the East in *Burmese Days*

[8] For Winston Smith, as for Flory before him, this seemingly grotesque performance is a lesson in comparative aesthetics. The singing woman is 'blown up to monstrous dimensions by childbearing', yet, Winston recognises, 'That's her style of beauty' (Orwell 1989c [1949]: 228). The lesson is also ethical

[9] It is arguable that Orwell's portrait of the snobbish and silly Elizabeth Lackersteen is misogynistic, although the male Europeans in the novel are nothing to write home about either

[10] Yeats's response to *Ubu* 'manages to combine aspects of disgust and wonder, fear and awe, distance and familiarity; all soon to be theorised by the Russian Formalists as "estrangement" and a little later by Brecht as the *Verfremdungseffect*' Taxidou (2007: 1)

[11] For example, Pablo Picasso was influenced by African art he saw displayed at the ethnographic museum of the Palais du Trocadéro in 1907, the year of *Les Demoiselles d'Avignon*. Antonin Artaud saw Balinese dance for the first time not in the East Indies but at the Colonial Exhibition in Paris in 1931

[12] 'Do away with the actor, and you do away with the means by which a debased stage-realism is produced and flourishes' (Craig 1908: 11). The actors in *Ubu Roi* had imitated the movements of marionettes and wore masks

[13] *Ostranenie*, the term from Russian Formalist criticism usually translated as 'defamiliarisation', has the literal meaning of 'making foreign'

[14] Matters so perfunctorily sketched here are explored more substantially in works such as Eksteins (1989), especially pp 9-54, Gay (2007), especially pp 231-280, Taxidou (2007) and Jones (2013)

[15] Such a description, to be sure, assimilates the *pwe* to a Western history and language and is inevitably as open to a charge of cultural appropriation as any other non-Burmese interpretation of it. There is no exit from the trap of Orientalism

[16] As seen above, the dancer observed by Norman Lewis, as soon as she had finished her piece, 'would suddenly relapse into a set pose, turn her back on the public, and squatting on her heels, make up her face or drink tea' (Lewis 1952: 28-29). No attempt is made to hide the artificiality of the performance or to pretend that it exists only in a dimension separate from everyday life

[17] The music of the *pwe* can seem cacophonous to an outsider. 'With goodwill and fair perseverance one can acquire a taste for this music, the keynote of which is unabashed vivacity' (Lewis 1952: 30)

[18] Susan Jones uses this phrase to describe Ezra Pound's interest in a 1919 production of *La Boutique Fantasque*, choreographed by Léonide Massine. In the ballet, dolls in a toyshop come to life

[19] 'For some the quest for a non-mimetic, non-psychological aesthetic that harbours abstraction and requires distance for appreciation finds something of a Holy Grail in the arts of the Orient' (Taxidou 2007: 119). 'The Marionette appears to me to be the last echo of some noble and beautiful art of a past civilization' (Craig 1908: 11)

[20] Early drafts that seem to be 'preliminaries to *Burmese Days*' are reproduced and discussed by Peter Davison. 'Whether they were written in Burma or shortly after Orwell's return from there, either in England or in France, is impossible to ascertain' (*CWGO* 10: 93-94)

[21] Orwell left Burma in July 1927 and settled in Paris in the spring of 1928. In 1928, Diaghilev was still director of the Ballets Russes in Paris

[22] The performance of the *pwe* is narrated in the novel, but in another frame of reference *Burmese Days* is itself a performance open to many kinds of spectation

REFERENCES

Bhabha, Homi (1985) Sly civility, *October*, Vol. 34 pp 71-80

Cannadine, David (2001) *Ornamentalism*, London: Allen Lane

Craig, Edward Gordon (1908) The actor and the Übermarionette, *Mask*, Vol. 1, No. 2 pp 3-15

Eksteins, Modris (1989) *Rites of Spring*, London: Bantam Press

Forster, E. M. (1979 [1924]) *A Passage to India*, Oliver Stallybrass (ed.), Harmondsworth: Penguin

Gay, Peter (2007) *Modernism: The Lure of Heresy from Baudelaire to Beckett and Beyond*, London: Heinemann

Jones, Susan (2013) *Literature, Modernism, and Dance*, Oxford: Oxford UP

Kerr, Douglas (2008) *Eastern Figures: Orient and Empire in British Writing*, Hong Kong: Hong Kong UP

Lewis, Norman (1952) *Golden Earth: Travels in Burma*, London: Jonathan Cape

Maung Htin Aung (1967) *A History of Burma*, New York: Columbia University Press

Orwell, George (1989a [1934]) *Burmese Days (BD)*, London: Penguin

Orwell, George (1989b [1938]) *Homage to Catalonia*, London: Penguin

Orwell, George (1989c [1949]) *Nineteen Eighty-Four*, London: Penguin

Orwell, George (1998) *The Complete Works of George Orwell (CWGO)*, 20 Vols, Davison, Peter (ed.) London: Secker & Warburg

Said, Edward W. (1978) *Orientalism*, Harmondsworth: Penguin

Taxidou, Olga (2007) *Modernism and Performance: Jarry to Brecht*, Basingstoke: Palgrave Macmillan

Taylor, D. J. (2003) *Orwell: The Life*, London: Chatto & Windus

Yeats, W. B. (1955 [1914]) The tragic generation, *Autobiographies*, London: Macmillan pp 279-349

NOTE ON THE CONTRIBUTOR

Douglas Kerr is Honorary Professor of English at the University of Hong Kong and Honorary Research Fellow at Birkbeck College, University of London. He is the author of *George Orwell* in the 'Writers and their Work' series (Northcote House, 2003). His other books are *Wilfred Owen's Voices* (Clarendon Press of Oxford University Press, 1993), *A Century of Travels in China* (co-edited, Hong Kong University Press, 2007), *Eastern Figures: Orient and Empire in British Writing* (Hong Kong University Press, 2008) and *Conan Doyle: Writing, Profession, and Practice* (Oxford University Press, 2013). His main current research interest is in Orwell and Asia.

Orwell, Poetry and the Microphone

TIM CROOK

This paper argues that poetry is an important preoccupation and reference point in George Orwell's identity as a writer – too often ignored. His first publication when a child was a jingoistic poem. It would seem his last draft of writing was a poem expressing the agonies of his declining body, dying and struggling for breath from tuberculosis. The publication in 2015 of a volume dedicated to his poems certainly pointed to the biographical significance of his poetic writing. This paper aims to demonstrate that there is an important connection between Orwell's criticism of poets and their poetry, the poetic cultural phenomenon, the potential of retrieving the oral tradition of poetry through broadcasting, as well as his own poetic expression. The analysis merits an artistic revaluation of the poetic Orwell and its relationship with his experience of radio broadcasting.

Keywords: poems, poetry, the microphone, broadcasting

THE POETIC 'JUGGLING ACT'

The growing cadre of Orwell biographers are not hugely appreciative of Orwell's poetic writings. For example, Jeffrey Meyers when quoting what I would regard as the impressive poem 'On a Ruined Farm near the [sic] His Master's Voice Gramophone Factory' describes it as 'rather labored' (Meyers 2001: 99). In one of the most influential English school texts on Orwell published in 1958, George Bott has nothing significant to say about Orwell's poetry output and even prefaces his long introduction with a poem by Robert Conquest *about* Orwell which contains, in my opinion, a highly contentious last verse (Bolt 1958: 1):

> While those who drown a truth's empiric part
> In dithyramb or dogma turn frenetic;
> Than whom no writer could be less poetic
> He left this lesson for all verse, all art.

Yet poetry runs through every genre of Orwell's writing output. He enchantingly juggles poems, poets and poetry into novels, essays,

TIM CROOK

quasi-autobiographical documentary, literary and cultural criticism, political analysis and satirical fable. He would jokingly quote Arnold Bennett: '… in the English-speaking countries the word "poetry" would disperse a crowd quicker than a fire hose' (Venables 2015: ix) when addressing its potential for the microphone. Poetry meant a huge amount to Orwell, but he always kept a mischievous sense of humour about it. For instance, when discussing the political propaganda in Charles Dickens' literary art he could not resist chiming that 'nearly everyone feels a sneaking affection for the patriotic poems that he learned by heart as a child. "Ye Mariners of England", "The Charge of the Light Brigade" and so forth. What one enjoys is not so much the poems themselves as the memories they call up' (Orwell and Angus 1970a, Vol. 1: 292).

Ironically, then, the first ever publication by the 11-year-old Eric Arthur Blair (George Orwell) on 2 October 1914 in *The Henley and South Oxfordshire Standard*, 'Awake! Young Men of England', has a scathing message for conscientious objectors, slackers and pacifists (Venables 2015: 1):

> For if, when your Country's in need
> You do not enlist by the thousand
> You truly are cowards indeed.

Dione Venables suggests this precocious work was the sensitive expression of a young lad sharing family grief and mourning for his first cousin, Neville Lascelles Ward, killed during the Battle of Mons in August 1914 (ibid: 2).

Even when talking about poverty and his personal sense of failure in his essay 'Why I Write' (1946) he was happy to recall and appreciate the little poem he composed in 1935 which opens and ends with two evocative stanzas (Orwell and Angus 1970a, Vol. 1: 28):

> A happy vicar I might have been
> Two hundred years ago,
> To preach upon eternal doom
> And watch my walnuts grow;
>
> ….
>
> I dreamed I dealt in marble halls,
> And woke to find it true;
> I wasn't born for an age like this;
> Was Smith? Was Jones? Were You?

This verse is in crystal clear language, with a simple traditional English rhyme and a meaning intensely charged with political irony.

It is poetry you can listen to, enjoy, feel and experience in mind, body and soul as if you were an intended audience of one. Trust Orwell to turn the art of poetry with window pane clarity and original political purpose, and more particularly for the purposes of this analysis, to write poetry elsewhere so euphonically for the radio medium.

Orwell had a lot to say about the uses and abuses of language as a medium of communication and his essay, perhaps written in 1940, 'New Words', is not as famous as 'Politics and the English Language', but it is certainly as infused with Orwellian fun. He is grappling with the 'utter incomprehension that exists between human beings – at least between those who are not deeply intimate' (Orwell and Angus 1970a, Vol. 2: 26). Before addressing the problem of deploying 'supposed appreciation of foreign poetry', Orwell sets us up with the exquisite and largely forgotten aphorism that perhaps deserves much greater emphasis and recognition in the dictionary of Orwellian quotations: 'Yet if words represented meanings as fully and accurately as height multiplied by base represents the area of a parallelogram, at least the necessity for lying would never exist' (ibid: 21). I can only say that my progress in O level Maths would have been so much more enjoyable had Orwell been my teacher.

Orwell wonders about the quite ignorant people, including himself, who derive vast pleasure out of poetry in foreign and even dead languages: 'I say to myself *Vixi puellis nuper idoneus*, and I repeat this over and over for five minutes for the beauty of the word *idoneus*' (ibid). The absurdity of uttering a Latin word when no one even knows how it should have been pronounced is the same as if he 'were in ecstasies over the beauty of a picture, and all because of some splashes of paint which had accidentally got on to the canvas two hundred years after it was painted' (ibid).

Orwell was an enthusiastic expert on 'good bad' poetry: he collected it with the same kind of pleasure he clearly derived from amassing Donald McGill's seaside postcards, the subject of his celebrated *Horizon* essay of 1941. Here, he finds the 'good' and 'bad' in Kipling's verse, declaring that most of it 'is so horribly vulgar that it gives one the same sensation as one gets from watching a third-rate music-hall performer recite "The Pigtail of Wu Fang Fu" with purple limelight on his face…' (ibid: 226). But then, having outraged retired Indian Army colonels and their memsahibs by tipping their Tiffin cucumber sandwiches to the floor, Orwell offers cream scones and strawberry jam by acknowledging that much of Kipling's poetry 'is capable of giving pleasure to people who know what poetry means' (ibid). He continues: 'At his worse, and also at his most vital, in poems like "Gunga Din" or "Danny Deever", Kipling is almost a shameful pleasure, like the taste for cheap sweets that some people secretly carry into middle life' (ibid).

TIM CROOK

ORWELL: THE 'QUIXOTIC MAN'

George Woodcock entitled his study of George Orwell *The Crystal Spirit* (1970): a key phrase that Dione Venables acknowledges was borrowed from the last line of one of Orwell's more memorable poems on the Italian soldier in the Spanish Civil War (Venables 2015: iii):

> No bomb that ever burst
> Shattered the crystal spirit.

Intriguingly, Woodcock did not fully engage in any literary criticism of Orwell's poetry. He did, however, recall the part that poetry performed in his everyday professional life at the BBC where they first met. Woodcock later said of his colleague that he was 'the nearest I had seen in real life to the imagined features of Don Quixote, and the rest of the figure went with the face. ... The resemblance to Don Quixote was appropriate, for in many ways Orwell can only be understood as an essentially quixotic man' (Woodcock 1970: 11).

Woodcock had been invited to take part in one of the BBC's wartime radio programmes on poetry that Orwell was pioneering while producing cultural propaganda to the young and university-educated native Indian elite of British India in 1942. Apart from being greeted by Orwell's 'flat-toned voice with a reserved but not unfriendly smile' (ibid: 12) Orwell lit up and positively disrupted the programme's preparation when (ibid: 14):

> ...he produced a volume of Byron and, smiling round at the rest of us, suggested that we should read 'The Isles of Greece' to show that English poets had a tradition of friendship for the aspirations of subject peoples. At that time the British government was opposed to the Indian Independence movement (Gandhi and Nehru were still in prison), but all of the participants in the broadcast supported it in sentiment at least, and as Herbert Read spoke the ringing verses of revolt, the programme assumed a mild flavour of defiance which we all enjoyed.

Here was evidence that Orwell's mission in poetry (as in the rest of his writing) had a political imperative. Orwell's first definitive biographer, Bernard Crick tracked this crucial aspect of his literary life. In the early days of childhood passion for Jacintha Buddicom, coincidentally a cousin of Dione Venables, Crick observed: 'Poetry was, indeed, to be important in the aspirations of both the boy and the man' (Crick 1992: 91). In his first chapter, 'As I was a chubby boy', the unfinished narrative poem about 'the plumber's daughter' found in one of his 1948 hospital notebooks inspires Crick's description of Orwell at this time (ibid: 45):

A sick and solitary man amuses himself by recalling his childhood and, despite the obvious irony of sky, stickleback and egg all being brighter, this is far from gloomy memory. There is no hint of sexual shame even, for it is quite clear that the 'deathly thing' is not his sexual encounter with, but his social rejection of the plumber's daughter: 'My mother says you're common.' Otherwise they simply 'played the games that all have played/ Though most remember not'. He was, indeed, a revolutionary in love with the Edwardian era. Certainly the verses refer to a time before he went to prep school as recounted in 'Such, Such Were the Joys'; but both accounts come from a mature man and are different perspectives on his own childhood. Who can say which was his dominant view, still less which was true? But it is likely that both happiness and misery were present.

Happiness and misery are the two curses that many clowns and poets have in common and throughout his life of writing Orwell has this charming ability to self-deprecate his skill and artistry in poetry with a delightfully apologetic, self-mocking tone.

Crick also identifies a certain insecurity and defensiveness about his identity as a poet when written to by an American librarian asking for manuscripts of his poems. Crick describes his reply as 'a sad admission that an old ambition had been abandoned' (Crick 1992: 368). Was he a poet 'whom it would be most unwise of us to neglect'? (ibid). Orwell replies: 'It might possibly have been Dylan Thomas or Rayner Heppenstall, both of whom I remember liked a poem of mine, or possibly it was Richard Rees. But anyway, I don't really write verse' (ibid).

He was being overly harsh with himself. The last poem he was writing when dying from the advanced stages of tuberculosis includes the poignant line 'Seven separate pains played in his body like an orchestra' (Venables 2015: 55). This is resonant, memorable and meaningful verse. Dione Venables adds that it 'is surely the most agonizingly revealing sentence that ever came from this brilliant and, by now, exhausted mind' (ibid).

RETRIEVING THE POETIC CANON

Before the publication of *George Orwell: The Complete Poetry*, as Dione Venables argues, very little of Orwell's poetry had been considered by the academy. She writes: 'He was not a major poet, and some might suggest that he was not even a minor one of any merit. But those critics would be wrong' (Venables 2015: i). Venables is also correct in ascribing much of the neglect about Orwell's poetry to the man himself. In a Preface, Professor Peter Davison, editor of the 20-volume *Collected Works*, presents a moving evaluation of Orwell's poetry by reference to his own life and experiences during the Second World War and argues that a

TIM CROOK

love of poetry never left Orwell. 'To the very end of his life he was attempting to write poetry' (ibid: v). Davison largely references the poems 'Awake! Young Men of England', 'On a Ruined Farm Near His Master's Voice Gramophone Factory', 'Memories of the Blitz', 'A Happy Vicar I Might Have Been' and 'The Italian Soldier'. But there is an overall critical tone: 'I do not doubt that my enjoyment and appreciation of Orwell as poet is to a large extent dictated by the personal associations some of his poems have for me – associations which, I confess, are irrelevant to the poetry in its own right' (ibid: xii).

Yet the poetic imperative in Orwell's writing output is far more than merely instrumental (as Davison suggests) to honing 'his skills as a master of prose' (ibid). The allegorical fable that is *Animal Farm* was written during the Second World War, a period marked by the most concentrated and impressive expression of Orwell's poetic writing blending the comic, ironic and the political. 'Beasts of England', composed and written by the character Major, an old prize Middle White boar, is to be sung to the fractured melodies of 'Clementine' and 'La Cucuracha':

> Soon or late the day is coming,
> Tyrant Man shall be o'erthrown,
> And the fruitful fields of England
> Shall be trod by beast alone.
>
> Rings shall vanish from our noses,
> And the harness from our back,
> Bit and spur shall rust forever,
> Cruel whips no more shall crack.

Animal Farm is the perfect prose novel for radio dramatisation. Orwell produced the first, for the BBC in 1947, and it has been revisited successfully by a number of later writers.

POETRY AND SOUND BROADCASTING

One of the most influential recent academic texts on poetry and the microphone is Professor Seán Street's *The Poetry of Radio: The Colour of Sound* (2012). Yet it does not have one reference to Orwell or his celebrated 1946 essay 'Poetry and the Microphone'. The major themes of the text – 'Sound as poem', 'Poets as radio', 'The poetry of the vernacular' – could easily have been linked to Orwell's profound insights expressed 66 years earlier. The tradition of the *Radio Ballads*, pioneered by D. G. Bridson, Charles Parker and Ewan McColl at the BBC, and Norman Corwin at CBS in the United States, deliberately combined verse and music, often with a clear political message. The verse plays of Louis MacNeice (BBC) and Archibald MacLeish (CBS, USA) explored the dramatic verse art-form in radio with seriousness and in the context of radio being the primary mass medium of electronic communication (McGann 1979).

Orwell's experience producing poetry programmes, giving poets a voice, using music as an accompaniment and stimulating discussions about the genre clearly inform his seminal essay, 'Poetry and the Microphone' which contains the wonderfully entertaining observation that 'Poetry on the air sounds like the Muses in striped trousers' (Orwell and Angus 1970b, Vol. 2: 380). Orwell was the producer who brought T. S. Eliot to the microphone for the first time actually voicing his poetry. The archive of Eliot reading poetry on the BBC, perhaps from a later broadcast, has been preserved, but nothing has survived of Orwell's own voice apart from a BBC memo discussing whether his voice was suitable for radio (BBC 1943). The Caribbean poet, Una Marson, and South Asian writers based in London at the time such as the poet M. J. Tambimuttu and novelist Mulk Raj Anand also read their work on Orwell's programmes.

Peter Davison believes Orwell's poetry programming for the BBC was not only fascinating, but innovative. Davison draws from the essay two key salient points (ibid ix). First he notes that 'the audience is conjectural, but it is an audience of one', or at most, a small group. Each listener will feel addressed individually. Further, the speaker – if possible the author – will soon realise that '*the audience has no power over you*'; the broadcaster does not have to take his tone from the audience – in effect to accommodate 'the stupidest person present'. There will be no need for the speaker to ingratiate himself or herself 'by means of the ballyhoo known as "personality"'.

Early on in his essay, Orwell emphasises that 'we had poems broadcast by the people who wrote them' (Orwell and Angus 1970b, Vol. 2: 374). The apologetic and mocking tone again appears. On the one hand he condemns the innovative magazine programme structure pioneered for the Indian service as 'slightly ridiculous and also rather patronizing' (ibid: 375) and at the same time makes it clear that the informal discussions were 'a lot less forbidding' and 'by such an approach you at least give a poem context, which is just what poetry lacks from the average man's point of view' (ibid).

Orwell mentions radio broadcasting as a means of popularising poetry while at the same time dismissing all his efforts and those of his colleagues as 'of no great value in themselves' (ibid: 376). Orwell was also fascinated by what poetry did for the poet and poetry as much as what radio did for poetry. His essay could have been retitled 'The Microphone and the Poet' instead (ibid):

TIM CROOK

I was early struck by the fact that the broadcasting of a poem by the person who wrote it does not merely produce an effect upon the audience, if any, but on the poet himself. One must remember that extremely little in the way of broadcasting poetry has been done in England, and that many people who write verse have never even considered the idea of reading it aloud. By being set down at a microphone, especially if this happens at all regularly, the poet is brought into a new relationship with his work, not otherwise attainable in our time and country.

'Poetry and the Microphone' was an important catalyst for Orwell in his explorations of the possibilities of poetry and radio broadcasting to retrieve the oral tradition for poets largely lost since the Gutenberg printing revolution. Indeed, his essay, it could be argued, helped inspire the regularly scheduled poetry radio programmes in Britain such as *Poetry Please* on BBC Radio 4 and *Words and Music* on BBC Radio 3.

Orwell suggests that printed poetry encourages obscurity and cleverness and has, consequently, become an art form for the elite. If it were to become normal to read verse aloud, then there is a potential 'democratisation' of the art form – to be realised through the medium of radio. Another special advantage for poetry on the radio, according to Orwell, is 'its power to select the right audience, and to do away with stage-fright and embarrassment' (ibid: 377). For Orwell, 'Poetry is disliked because it is associated with unintelligibility. Intellectual pretentiousness and a general feeling of Sunday-on-a-weekday. Its name creates in advance the same sort of bad impression as the word "God", or a parson's dog-collar' (ibid). Orwell is being evangelical here. This essay was intended to be a cultural manifesto to make poetry accessible for the 'big public' (ibid): 'It is a question of getting people to listen instead of uttering a mechanical raspberry.'

The last two pages of the essay engage with the contemporary politics of broadcasting during World War Two. Davison suspects it was written in 1943 with publication in the *New Saxon Pamphlet* in March 1945. In short, Orwell urges governments to make verse and poetry on the radio rather than propaganda.

CONCLUSION

There is no doubt that at various times in his life Orwell harboured a strong ambition to write poetry and perhaps he also hoped that he would achieve some recognition for it. He continued to write poems and was an avid reader and critic right to the end of his life. He shared a self-consciousness and lack of confidence about his own poetic identity that he also identified as the cultural problem confronting this most refined of literary art forms. In radio, he discovered a revolutionary opportunity to democratise it.

Significantly, Orwell never advanced his status as a major poet – nor as a writer who should be recognised for his poetry. His status as a poet developed from his experience as a poetry producer in BBC radio broadcasting and the presence of his poetic voice in his prose. He gave voice to poetry's potential in broadcasting and this would certainly not have been possible had it not been for his personal love of poetry and the experience of writing it.

REFERENCES

BBC (1943) Memo criticising Orwell's voice, BBC Archive: Orwell at the BBC, Available online at http://www.bbc.co.uk/archive/orwell/7427.shtml, accessed on 31 October 2018

Bott, George (ed.) (1958) *George Orwell: Selected Writings*, London: Heinemann Educational

Crick, Bernard (1992) *George Orwell: A Life*, Harmondsworth, Middlesex: Penguin Books

Davison, Peter (1998) *The Complete Works of George Orwell, Vol. 17, I Belong to the Left 1945*, London: Secker & Warburg

Orwell Sonia and Angus, Ian (1970a) *The Collected Essays, Journalism and Letters of George Orwell, Vol. 1, An Age Like This 1920-1940*, Harmondsworth, Middlesex: Penguin Books

Orwell Sonia and Angus, Ian (1970b) *The Collected Essays, Journalism and Letters of George Orwell, Vol. 2, My Country Right or Left*, Harmondsworth, Middlesex: Penguin Books

McGann, Mary Evelyn (1979) *Voices from the Dark: A Study of the Radio Achievement of Norman Corwin, Archibald MacLeish, Louis MacNeice, Dylan Thomas, and Samuel Beckett*, PhD. dissertation, University of Indiana, USA

Meyers, Jeffrey (2001) *Orwell: Wintry Conscience of a Generation*, New York/London: W. W. Norton & Company

Street, Seán (2012) *The Poetry of Radio: The Colour of Sound*, Abingdon, Oxon: Routledge

Venables, Dione (2015) *George Orwell: The Complete Poetry*, England: Finlay Publishing for The Orwell Society

Woodcock, George (1970) *The Crystal Spirit: A Study of George Orwell*, Harmondsworth, Middlesex: Penguin Books

NOTE ON THE CONTRIBUTOR

Tim Crook is a Professor in the Department of Media, Communications and Culture at Goldsmiths, University of London, Visiting Professor of Broadcast Journalism at Birmingham City University and Vice-President of the Chartered Institute of Journalists. He has written chapters and academic articles on the literature and journalism of George Orwell and he is currently completing a study for Ashgate/Routledge, *George Orwell On The Radio*.

SHORT STORY

2017 My Year of Orwell – and *One Last Gift*

Nicola Rossi explains how The Orwell Society's Student Fiction Competition inspired her to start writing stories, and explores the social, political and technological context for One Last Gift, *published below.*

I have come to view 2017 as my year of Orwell. I was studying in London, and frequently found myself walking through Deptford. I stayed at a hotel in Paris. I became involved in a violent struggle in Barcelona with a mugger on a moped. I ended up changing trains in Wigan, somewhere I'd never been before in my life in spite of growing up less than 20 miles away.

To cap it all, I found myself in a hospital in the South of France, looking after someone who had been struck unexpectedly with appendicitis. For her, that was 'the worst thing in the world', and the number on the door to her ward was, of course, 101.

Most importantly though, for me in 2017, I was inspired to start writing fiction again by The Orwell Society, whose student dystopian fiction competition gave me a new focus, and boosted my confidence in my creative abilities. The short story I entered (below) has now become the basis for a novel, *Rock Star Ending*, which I completed over the summer. It is now with literary agents for consideration.

It all began one afternoon in the Professor Stuart Hall Building at Goldsmiths, where I was studying for an MA in Digital Media. Sitting in the coffee bar between lectures, I looked up from my Foucault and caught a glimpse of one of the ubiquitous information screens. Instead of Big Brother looking down on me, however, I saw George Orwell's kindly face next to a strip of copy inviting entries for the competition. I knew instantly what I wanted to write about. Something that had been on my mind for many years, but for which I had never found an outlet. In the footsteps of Orwell (1970a [1946]), I was going to try to make 'political writing into an art'.

RULES FOR EFFECTIVE WRITING

Before the competition, and the permission it gave me to begin my journey experimenting with the dystopian genre, Orwell had already given me some excellent career guidance.

I have worked for 30 years in corporate communications, doing PR for big businesses. For many that may seem like a dystopian nightmare in itself, although that wasn't my experience. Orwell was relevant to my career simply because good writing is the foundation of all PR, as it is of journalism. To be successful, I had to develop a straightforward writing style, succinct and clear. I often reminded myself and my colleagues about Orwell's rules for effective writing, in 'Politics and the English Language' (1970b [1946]), when striving to come up with something a journalist might actually want to read and follow up on.

When I worked at BT in the 1990s the company won awards for making its 'terms and conditions' (Ts & Cs) readable and simple. If only the Ts & Cs of the 21st century were designed in the same way. Joseph Turow, of the Annenberg School of Communication, says he has been informed by 'lawyers who write the policies for large organisations' that these days they are simply 'not designed to be understood by ordinary people' (2015).

Moreover, flick through the blogs, LinkedIn posts, annual reports and tweets of any tech firm, and you will find technological utopian motifs in abundance. The promise of a better life through technology is rife among the tech giants who dominate much of our popular culture. Pressure on communicators and journalists to pour fuel on the fire of hype can sometimes be overwhelming, and ever-more exaggerated claims emerge every day.

ARTIFICIAL INTELLIGENCE AND THE SINGULARITY

A primary theme for my writing is how Artificial Intelligence (AI) could be used to manipulate people into making decisions with terminal consequences. The *Economist* (2018) has described AI as: '... much more than another Silicon Valley buzzword – more, even, than seminal products like the smartphone. It is better seen as a resource, a bit like electricity, that will touch every part of the economy and society'.

In the past year, the UK government has set up a Centre for Data Ethics and Innovation[1] and the AI for Good Foundation[2] has been established in the US, both with honourable intentions to help society benefit from this powerful computing technology. Meanwhile, the application of AI is streaking ahead, being activated in everything from autonomous weapons, to self-driving cars, to predicting whether children are likely to be abused (McIntyre and Pegg 2018).

NICOLA ROSSI

I am in good company when worrying about possible misuses of AI. Stephen Hawking, the internationally acclaimed theoretical physicist, cosmologist and author, was among a group of scientists who co-authored an article in the *Independent* questioning the likely benefits of 'the singularity', the time in the future when artificial intelligence might reign supreme (Hawking et al. 2014). They concluded with the punchline: 'Success in creating AI would be the biggest event in human history. Unfortunately, it might also be the last, unless we learn how to avoid the risks.' Furthermore, the excellent book by Cathy O'Neil (2016), *Weapons of Math Destruction*, explains how the software that increasingly manages our lives encodes prejudice and bias into the system. As a result, according to O'Neil, mathematical models at work in areas such as financial services tend to make the rich richer, and discriminate against people who are poor and oppressed.

How much time have we left to get on top of this phenomenon? Ray Kurzweil, Google's chief engineer and renowned futurologist, has predicted the singularity will happen 'within the next 30 years' (Galeon and Reed 2017). In the context of the history of the planet, it's a blink away.

DON'T STOP THE 'TERMINATOR' CHAT

The Leverhulme Centre for the Future of Intelligence[3] and the Royal Society have jointly commissioned the AI Narratives Project, recognising that the evolution of the story of complex, novel technologies is inextricably linked with its technical development. How AI is depicted in culture and the media influence how regulation and public opinion play out. My blood ran cold at the CogX18 conference in London this year, however, when one of the AI narratives project team members included in her presentation the remark: 'We have to stop the *Terminator* chat.' 'No!' I tweeted. 'Imagining the worst is fundamental to avoiding it.'

My story is set in the near future, long before the time when the singularity is predicted to occur. It is not concerned with machines staging a *Terminator*-style take over. I am more anxious about the damage a handful of people with concentrated power could do – probably by accident – instructing machines to do terrible things, surreptitiously, without the rest of us realising what is happening.

Some would say this is already taking place. Witness the ever-lengthening queue of former Facebook and Google employees setting up institutes and pressure groups such as the US-based Center for Humane Technology, which wants '…to realign technology with humanity's best interests'[4] It is disconcerting that the people who have seen inside the tech superpowers have become adamant that much of what they are doing is damaging society.

With machines mediating between the organisation and the individual, the sense of human responsibility can become diluted. There are fewer people in the chain of command to blow the whistle if an anonymous developer, somewhere, programmes an invisible, malign algorithm and sets it free.

With this in mind, my story questions whether it is possible for people to tell the difference between choice and manipulation in an increasingly data-driven world. It also explores the social and political circumstances that might lead ordinary people to bring about the premature demise of their fellow human beings, and – more optimistically – what might inspire them to help each other carry on.

One Last Gift

SHORT STORY

Happy birthday to me. I've made it to 85. Lived longer than both my parents, three of my grandparents, and all those musicians who died at 27. Jim Morrison, Janis Joplin, Amy Winehouse – you probably don't know them. It was a while ago. Maybe you've heard of David Bowie or George Michael? They lasted quite a bit longer, and I've outlived them too.

I used to want the words 'Never a Dull Moment' to be chiselled on to my gravestone. However, I went off the idea as it gradually became obvious that it would be misleading. Once I got past that magical 27 years old, things calmed down considerably. I think that's how it is for a lot of people. It's not that I haven't packed a lot in over the years, but so much of life is mundane, isn't it?

At the end of the last century they told us that my generation would live longer than any of the preceding ones. I was aiming to crash through the 100 barrier. I took up weight training to stave off muscle wastage, and ate lots of kale to prevent cancer. I still feel pretty good. But like most other things in life it comes down to what's practical. Soon it will all be over. I'm not going to get a headstone either. They don't really do them for people like me.

It shouldn't have come as a surprise. The shift was bound to happen. Or should I call it the shaft? Old people have never really been valued here, but at least we used to be protected because we voted more than anyone else. It wasn't in anyone's interests to upset us. But then after Brexit the Millennials began to wake up, realised they outnumbered us, and decided they didn't want to pay for us anymore.

NICOLA ROSSI

There was a debate in parliament about what they called the maturity premium. How it wasn't fair that younger people couldn't afford homes, jobs, health care – that sort of thing – when some older people were quite comfortable. I can see where they were coming from. Unfortunately though, they decided that the only way to make ends meet was to siphon all the wealth from the old and give it to the young. What made an even more compelling case was that, when immigration was stopped, they simply couldn't get enough cheap people from other places in the world to prop up the hospitals and care homes the old people relied on.

I could get mad about it if I let myself. It's true, I do have a house even if it is a bit cold and dilapidated these days. But it's not as if I didn't work hard for it. I came to this city with nothing, slowly paid off my debts, and finally got reasonably comfortable. So what if my house is worth a million pounds? To me it's just somewhere to live. I certainly don't feel like a millionaire. I'm just someone who's done OK over the years and been able to raise my family without ever asking the state to help.

I'm beginning to sound a bit resentful. If I was going to get hung up on the detail I'd also mention that I did all of this whilst paying a huge amount of tax. I had always thought paying taxes was right. So it felt like a massive kick in the teeth when the government decided they no longer wanted to do anything for anyone once they reached 85.

So it's not really a happy birthday to me at all. From today I no longer qualify for any state support. No subsidised medical care. No free prescriptions. No state pension. No free TV licence. Even my bus pass has to go back. I could cover some of the costs myself, as least for a while. But that's not the point. What hurts the most is that in the eyes of the state I feel I am worth nothing – nothing apart from the One Last Gift I'll be giving later this afternoon.

Like many other cons of neoliberalism, today's activity is cloaked under the guise of choice. With One Last Gift, I can choose from a range of carefully designed options detailing how and when I want the state to kill me. This is how it works.

First of all you get your unique login to the One Last Gift portal. You put in your national insurance number and your tax reference so they can be certain who you are. Then you have to do a sort of online quiz to prove that you are capable of making The Big Decision. I heard they paid a fortune to make the interface as simple and user-friendly as possible. I'm sure you can guess who designed the algorithm.

The questions are what you'd expect. IQ and memory tests which they match to everything they've scraped from the net about you over the years. They have to make sure you are of sound mind if you are going to be making important life and death decisions. I still find it amazing how much they know about me, even now. Once you pass the test you can go on to make your other choices. I was really pleased that I scored 86 per cent positive with a dementia quotient of 3.2 per cent in the 'negligible' range. In other circumstances passing with those flying colours would be good news.

The online will section is great. You don't need to see a solicitor anymore, just fill in the form and it gets countersigned by a legal executive in a few seconds. No need for expensive lawyers or probate or the mountain of admin we had to plough through when our parents died. You can even arrange for your bills to stop at the moment of death on a page sponsored by the utility companies.

Then you go on to the Departure Board. This part can be quite upsetting but a little chat window pops up and someone – or it might be a bot, I can never tell these days – helps you along. They reassure you that you're doing the right thing, that the next generation will be forever grateful, that you are sparing your children seeing you die a horrible painful death in abject poverty smeared in your own excrement. Well, that got me over the line. On to the Options Screen.

SHORT STORY

I would have preferred to die at home, in my own environment. I've lived in this house for forty years. My children grew up here, my grandchildren have played in the garden, I grew old in comfort. But I decided against it. It's the most expensive option because they need a team to look after you when they give you the drugs, and then they need to take your body away for disposal afterwards. It all adds up. Not to mention the insurance. They actually employ real people to do these At Home Peaceful Endings, although I've heard there is a robotic option being trialled in Scotland at the moment which will be cheaper. But that would be too late for me. The other problem with doing it at home would be that people might notice the Peaceful Endings waggon outside the house and try to interfere. Worse, they might even call one of the children. Far better it just comes as a surprise, with the money and the house as a consolation prize.

I could have gone for the no-frills package. With that one, the council sends a communal bus to take you to your local disposal centre, along with the rest of the day's customers. There's a lot of demand, so they are re-using the vehicles they once used to ferry people with special needs to schools and day centres. They called people 'service-users' then. That was before all the social care stopped.

NICOLA ROSSI

The big difference, of course, is that this is a one way ticket. They take care of the economy out-goers in a medical annex next to the crematorium. It keeps the transport costs down and is good for the environment. It all looks very calm and humane from the videos. But that option is meant for people with no next of kin, no money and no alternative. A bit like the old pauper's funeral. Not for me. I thought to myself, if you can't spoil yourself on your last day on earth, when can you?

So I pulled all the stops out and went for the Rock Star Option. It's being run by one of the airlines. In my day most rock stars – lots of those 27-year-olds actually – died in a hotel room after a big party. A lot of them seemed to choke on their own vomit. This isn't like that. It feels is a bit more like what happened to Michael Jackson. I'm older than he was too, incidentally. He passed away in his luxury mansion after one too many doses of dodgy general anaesthetic.

When I was an executive I used to love flying Business Class. A chauffeur came to my house, took me to a private entrance to the airport, and I was fast-tracked through security and check-in. I always arrived early to make time for eggs benedict, a manicure and a mohito in the lounge before getting on the plane. How I loved meeting people all over the world, sleeping on a flat-bed in the air, and watching all those films. Changing into free branded pyjamas. They even had luxury chocolate to snack on and little pots of hipster-inspired ice cream. From what I can tell on the portal, the Rock Star Endings service is similar. They wouldn't give their brand to something that wasn't a lovely experience and risk their reputation, would they?

Obviously the arrangements have to be a bit different. They can't take you to a glamorous lounge full of other high flyers, as you might change your mind or create a scene. And you probably don't feel like eggs benedict either. But there is a lovely soft bed and enormous playlist which is curated by guest celebrities to ease you out gently. If you want you can even wear a VR headset that leads you towards an afterlife scenario of your choice. I won't bother with that. They only make me feel seasick.

The car they send for you is driverless naturally, but a Peaceful Endings Angel comes to your house to escort you to the departure lounge. An actual person who has been specially trained. They pop in an hour before you're due to leave to help calm any last minute nerves. Given the massive drive to get people to 'move on', the government has waived some of the regulations around controlled drugs, and they will give you something to make it easier to close your door one last time. In fact, you have to commit to taking the special cocktail of medication within ten minutes of their arrival at your home when you sign up. And there's also the big nappy –

to spare embarrassment. Then they walk with you to the car and make sure your house is secure and that the keys go to your next of kin as soon as the procedure is over. To passers-by, it just looks like you're getting into a taxi.

It must be a funny job, collecting people to go for disposal. There isn't much conventional nursing work around these days, not since the medi-robots took off. So they don't have any trouble getting people to do it. I've heard the pay's good. Still, I can't be the first person to think of them as the angel of death. Probably best not to say that to them when they arrive, just in case they turn. They probably get it all the time.

I worry how the kids will feel when they've found out that I opted-in to the opt-out. They are so far away. Since being priced out of London they have had to move to other continents to establish their own lives. They might be angry with me at first, but in the long run I think they'll be glad to have been spared the burden of having to fly back to deal with various old age crises as I gradually deteriorate. As they say on the portal: 'One Last Gift is an act of love.' Heart emoji.

SHORT STORY

The fun part is that I've been able to design my own memorial webpage and remembrance ritual. My body will be incinerated and the ashes stored for six months. If no-one collects them after that time they'll go to landfill. If they want, the kids can have something fancy done with my ashes – up to 12 paperweights or statuette can be 3D printed to order. I could have advance-purchased them but I didn't want to burden people with tat. I can hear the arguments now: 'No we can't throw that away, it's Grandma.'

The music for the service is chanting from a yoga class I used to do. I spent years trying to persuade my family to come to yoga with me, but they never would. Perhaps they'll find it calming. I always did. I've edited some subtitles translating the Sanskrit so they know it's all about peace and that kind of thing. For a moment I considered asking them to play David Bowie's *Rock 'n' Roll Suicide*, but I couldn't stop crying when I listened to the lyrics.

Once I'd decided to go ahead it took about an hour to complete the booking. In the end, it was the *85 bonanza* incentive that really clinched it. It's an amazing deal. If you book your exit to take place on or before your 85th birthday you get a 50 per cent discount on the fees. More importantly, though, there is tax break on your estate which exempts everything you leave behind from inheritance tax. That will mean the kids get a much better pay-out. It was a no-brainer really. These days you can make all these decisions on your own without your family's consent. It must save a lot of arguments.

NICOLA ROSSI Once you've covered all the details you have to pay by bank transfer. It's just in case your credit card statement date is after you've gone and they don't get the money. There's the usual terms and conditions. I actually read them for once and ticked all the boxes even though the cancellation policy was extremely disturbing. Once you get past the mandatory two-weeks cooling-off period, it's non-existent. Like one of those gangster films when you pay a hit man who then won't let you change your mind.

Not long to go now. I'd better eat something. The Angel isn't due for another couple of hours. All my life I've been trying to eat less, and on the one day when it doesn't matter if I get fat I don't really feel like it. I've been running down the fridge and the freezer. Took everything from the cupboards that was still in date to the food bank. I've kept an egg aside though. I'll boil it for five minutes. That's always nice. Bit of salt. Butter. Cup of tea. I've always thought that the simple things make it good to be alive. Better make the most of it. That jam doughnut can go in the bin. It seemed like a good idea when I bought it, but I don't fancy it now.

NOTES

[1] Centre for Data Ethics and Innovation. See online at https://www.gov.uk/government/consultations/consultation-on-the-centre-for-data-ethics-and-innovation, accessed on 21 September 2018

[2] AI for Good. See online at https://ai4good.org/, accessed on 21 September 2018

[3] Leverhulme Centre for the Future of Intelligence. See online at http://lcfi.ac.uk/projects/ai-narratives-and-justice/ai-narratives/, accessed on 21 September 2018

[4] Center for Humane Technology, See online at http://humanetech.com/, accessed on 21 September 2018

REFERENCES

Economist (2018) How Europe can improve the development of AI, 20 September. Available online at https://www.economist.com/leaders/2018/09/22/how-europe-can-improve-the-development-of-ai, accessed on 21 September 2018

Galeon, Dom and Reed, Christianna (2017) Kurzweil claims that the singularity will happen by 2045, *Futurism*, 5 October. Available online at https://futurism.com/kurzweil-claims-that-the-singularity-will-happen-by-2045/, accessed on 21 September 2018

Hawking, Stephen, Russell, Stuart, Tegmark, Max and Wilczek, Frank (2014) Transcendence looks at the implications of artificial intelligence – but are we taking AI seriously enough? *Independent,* 1 May. Available online at https://www.independent.co.uk/news/science/stephen-hawking-transcendence-looks-at-the-implications-of-artificial-intelligence-but-are-we-taking-9313474.html, accessed on 21 September 2018

McIntyre, Niamh and Pegg, David (2018) Councils use 377,000 people's data in efforts to predict child abuse, *Guardian*, 16 September. Available online at https://www.theguardian.com/society/2018/sep/16/councils-use-377000-peoples-data-in-efforts-to-predict-child-abuse, accessed on 21 September 2018

O'Neil, Cathy (2016) *Weapons of Math Destruction: How Big Data Increases Inequality and Threatens Democracy,* New York: Crown Publishing Group

Orwell, George (1970a [1946]) Why I Write, Orwell, Sonia and Angus, Ian (eds) *The Collected Essays, Journalism and Letters, Vol. 1*: Harmondsworth, Middlesex: Penguin Books pp 23-30. First published in *Gangrel,* No. 4

Orwell, George (1970b [1946]) Politics and the English language, Orwell, Sonia and Angus, Ian (eds) *The Collected Essays, Journalism and Letters, Vol. 4*: Harmondsworth, Middlesex: Penguin Books pp 156-169. First published in *Horizon*, April

Turow, Joseph, Hennessy, Michael and Draper, Nora (2015) *The Tradeoff Fallacy: How Marketers Are Misrepresenting American Consumers and Opening Them Up to Exploitation*, Philadelphia: University of Pennsylvania Press

NOTE ON THE CONTRIBUTOR

After graduating from UCL in English Literature, Nicola Rossi spent three decades managing corporate communications for technology companies. In 2017, she took a sabbatical to complete an MA in Digital Media at Goldsmiths University. While there, her story, *One Last Gift,* came runner up in the Orwell Society Dystopian Fiction Competition. Nicola has now completed her first novel, *Rock Star Ending*, which expands on the premise of her competition entry.

SHORT STORY

ARTICLE

'Room 103': Orwell's Influence on Contemporary Visual Art

GLENN IBBITSON

The freedom of the individual to think independently of state permissions was the founding principle of George Orwell's writings. Perhaps this is why so many visual artists identify with his work. Although he himself was not a visual artist and art criticism does not figure prominently in his work, artists respond to his intellectual honesty in these times in which their activities are seen as a 'soft option', and honest political analysis is denigrated as 'fake news'. Over the last several months, I have been engaged in numerous discussions about Orwell and the prescience of his ideas. These conversations have encouraged me to construct 'Room 103': a blog-site where makers and those engaged in time-based visual media can present work engaging with 'Orwellian' themes. The wide range of their contributions testifies to the continuing relevance of the writer's oeuvre to visual culture.

Keywords: Orwell, contemporary art, surveillance, online profiling, repression, Saul Hay Gallery

THE CORRIDOR LEADING TO ROOM 103

The source for 'Room 103: A visual tribute to George Orwell' can be traced back to my adolescence, where I constructed for myself a pantheon of heroes. You probably did the same. This eclectic and constantly altering accumulation included sundry artists, writers, sportsmen and historical figures, including Lincoln, Gandhi, Robert. E. Lee and Douglas Bader. Of this large, early company, eroded through subsequent processes of revisionist education drawing on more informed sources, only three reputations now remain intact; Ernest Shackleton, Joseph Frank (Buster) Keaton and George Orwell. Of these three, only Orwell's name crops up unprompted in media conversation on a weekly, and sometimes daily, basis. It may be misused by people who are referencing anything remotely dystopian or anti-social, but for me, that still provides some valuable measure of the length of shadow this man's work throws across the landscape of contemporary thought.

I suppose one of the reasons people refer to Orwell in reference to my art is that the themes I pursue invite the comparison. I tend to focus my work on subjects which Orwell interrogated through his writings: surveillance, state controls, corporate influence, restrictions on individual liberty, limitations on thought. As Orwell has set the conversational pattern at exhibition previews for several years now, diverting attention from both the art on the walls and the free bar, I decided last year to test the waters and propose a tribute to him. This would take the form of an online gallery blog, where like-minded artists could display any work reflecting Orwellian themes, or art which in some way bears the influence of his writing. From the beginning, I saw this as a virtual window display to attract the attention of a bricks and mortar gallery.

I called this particular plot in cyberspace 'Room 103'. The title follows on from Room 101 where Winston Smith, the anti-hero of Orwell's dystopian masterpiece *Nineteen Eighty-Four* (1949), is tortured. It was actually situated in 55 Portland Place, and not in Broadcasting House, as is commonly thought. And there Orwell was forced to attend far too many deadly dull meetings. I imagined the arts programmes being planned two doors down the corridor, in Room 103. Now, you may justifiably label me as the artist who put the lie in artistic licence and to that charge I plead guilty. But then we all crave a catchy title after all…

CRITERIA FOR ENTRY INTO 'ROOM 103'

Reference to Orwell's work makes for a very wide brief open to interpretation – exactly the intellectual climate artists prefer. I wanted the blog-site to reflect this potential for variety and decided whenever possible to accept submissions without bringing my personal aesthetic preferences into play. Artists face neither strict selection processes nor a list of restrictions. I am happier playing the role of enabler rather than that of judge. The only three submissions I have rejected made no mention anywhere of George Orwell. I do consider this a 'red line'.

Traditional techniques are presented alongside time-based media. I have imposed no limit on the field of activity. Indeed, one of the contributors regards himself rather more of a poet than a photographer, while another is developing a performance career beyond her sculptural practice.

There is no age or experience restriction; student work is as welcome as that from established talent. I make it a policy to look at the work before any accompanying curriculum vitae material.

Submissions may be works in progress; finished works will be added at a later date, as the artist's page remains open to updated information.

GLENN IBBITSON

A brief statement on how Orwell has had an influence on a particular project or practice in general accompanies the images.

We live in times when artists are used by galleries and institutions as cash-cows. When I was a recently graduated painter, exhibition opportunities, which charged before selection, were the exception; now entry fees are the general rule. I tend not to submit under such conditions; I don't expect other makers to have to do so. I determined that the initial submission stage should be free. When a venue is found, a hanging fee might be imposed, but only to cover expenses, insurance and publicity, and will be kept to a minimum. This is not designed as a money-making exercise.

PRELIMINARY ONLINE PUBLICITY

Online promotion is the key to any website's success. The first advertising posters were derived from a suite of unique, one-off screen-prints. These form part of a design proposal for a series of covers for Orwell's titles. They have been based on both the graphic and physical qualities derived from the over-layerings, degradation and tearing or ripping of posters from billboards. Orwell's finest writing for me has the graphic power and universal clarity of communication one finds in the best poster art. These prints were publicly previewed in May 2017 at 'PrintFest', an exhibition of contemporary printmaking which is held annually in the Coronation Hall, at Ulverston, Cumbria. From there, they were shipped to a private collector in Albuquerque, New Mexico. I am delighted that they form part of a cultural protest on the front line against the doublespeak currently emanating from the White House.

CONTRIBUTORS: PATRIOTISM AND SOCIETY

Tony Baker

A stylistic influence on these posters was the work of Tony Baker. He is the artist who more than any other encouraged me to press ahead with this project. He was the first to submit work to the project and has acted as recruiting officer thereafter – in both Spain and the UK. I first met him at a talk he gave as part of the 21st International Contemporary Book Art Fair, in Leeds, in 2017. He presented his recent collection, *Homage to Homage to Catalonia* (2015), a book of 297 images that contrast Orwell's nation caught in the middle of a civil war with that of a present day Catalonia which, at the time of publication, was in the process of re-assessing its identity through an Independence referendum (declared illegal by the Spanish government). Through its juxtaposition of photography, typography and digital printmaking, the book explores the culture and fabric of a country that still has democracy and republicanism flowing through its veins. The photographs and digital prints sit side-by-side with four-line poems based on Orwell's text, that appear like the residue of slogans found daubed on the walls and street furniture of both the past and present day Catalonia.

Paul Steffan Jones

Paul Steffan Jones is a photographer poet whose work also looks to *Homage to Catalonia* through the optic of a genealogy project which revealed a veteran of the International Brigade in his family.

Thomas Isaac Picton was a miner. When the Great War broke out in 1914, he enlisted and stayed working with coal, becoming a stoker in the Royal Navy, fighting at Jutland in May 1916. In the 1920s, in a country which failed to meet its obligations to the volunteers and conscripted civilian forces who had saved it, he became a boxer. Steffan Jones writes: 'He managed to get a small number of professional bouts but was primarily a bare knuckle mountain fighter. At least one of his confrontations led him to prison. On one occasion, he left Cardiff jail after serving a short sentence for assaulting a police officer, wearing the boots of a prisoner who had recently been hanged.'

Tom joined the International Brigade in his mid-40s, older than the typical volunteer; swapping one set of uncertainties: those blighting the Welsh industrial zone, for another – Spain at war with itself. Steffan Jones adds: 'He fought in the Battle of Teruel and was captured soon after and imprisoned in Bilbao. He was murdered by his jailers in April 1938 after he had punched a guard who was beating a fellow prisoner with his rifle butt. The *Rhondda Leader* newspaper of 29 October 1938 reported that he had been put up against a wall and shot. His body was never found. This is my tribute to him:

> **Icons**
>
> Not game footage
> but I've outlived Stanley Baker
> as non-pacifist fist anti-fascist
> in humidity following Biblical rainfall
> we all rust

Antoni Garcia Serrat

Antoni Garcia Serrat is a young artist based in Barcelona. He writes:

> Although I have read George Orwell's work I cannot claim to be an expert on his writings. I remember that the reading of *Nineteen Eighty-Four* had a great impact on me. His vision of a kind of controlled society was highly prescient and has had a depressive effect on my vision about the role of the individual on contemporary society. I think that nowadays many countries close their doors to save themselves but instead they only make prisoners of their citizens. The artist Tony Baker led me to recover my interest in George Orwell through his exhibition and lecture at the Art School of Catalonia last year. As a Catalan citizen I

am very grateful to George Orwell for aiding the fight against fascism and for his work *Homage to Catalonia*, especially at this moment when our rights as a country are threatened.

The imagery presented in Serrat's work evokes an unquantifiable menace, stalking his nation's past and present: interior spaces where corridors and staircases disappear into shadow; where bad things can happen…

Kerry Baldry

There is no such room for conjectures with the film, *Boot*, by Kerry Baldry. The bad thing is already happening – and it is happening to you, the viewer. As Orwell wrote in *Nineteen Eighty-Four*: 'If you want a vision of the future, imagine a boot stamping on a human face – forever.' Shot from a subjective viewpoint, the viewer only sees the underside of the jackboot – occasionally stamping noisily and viciously, through 1 minute and 25 seconds of blank screen.

Baldry's films have been screened on BBC2's *The Late Show*, at the Institute of Contemporary Arts in London, at the Rotterdam Film Festival and as part of Empire II Venice Biennale in 2017.

Mary M. Mazziotti

Mary M. Mazziotti is a visual artist working in Pittsburg, California, who practises hand-embroidery on textiles, reflecting a special interest in contemporary socio-political *memento mori*. She writes:

> Like so many artists, my work was galvanized by our 2016 election in the USA and the subsequent inversion of honour, truth and decency in government. Now Lies are Truth and Truth is Fake News. 'Needling the Regime' is my imagining what official state-sanctioned art would look like in American Oceania. It primarily combines images from vintage propaganda posters (Soviet, Nazi, Maoist, American) with text from Comrade Trump and his myrmidons, as well as the occasional prescient Orwellian quote.

Paul Salt and Sue Shaw

Salt and Shaw collaborate on the production of unique or small edition, hand-crafted book art. Their contribution is still at the research stage. They write:

> 'On Location' is a proposal in response to George Orwell's experience of our home city of Sheffield which, he wrote in *The Road to Wigan Pier* (1937), 'could justly claim to be the ugliest town in the Old World'. At that time, our parents were toddlers and our grandparents were miners, labourers and domestics; facing unemployment as they raised a family; taking in washing to make ends meet. Our lives have been very different to theirs, escaping to the 'big city' of Sheffield, where the art college took

us on a journey away from the pits, steelworks and factories that could have ensnared us. Now we find ourselves in a region where heavy industries have almost disappeared, leaving only a few traces of what once thrived. Pit wheels stand as monuments to mines closed in the 1980s. A shopping centre has crouched over the site of the Edgar Allen Foundry since 1990. In 2001, a museum opened, in what was once the world's largest steel plant, to show how record-breaking amounts of steel were made; but without the necessary heat, labour and danger or production.

How do we find South Yorkshire in 2018? What remains and what has changed? Have these unreported places fallen from public attention and concern – conveniently disappearing, in fact? What has happened to the landscape and topography; the re-use of space, the removal and replacement of industry?

How will we respond once out 'On Location'? What do our past connections and present links mean to us? What will we discover, write about and record? How can this gathered material be used to produce a new artists' book?

In both a personal and political exploration, we will be looking for the clues and details just beneath the surface of the contemporary urban landscapes on our doorstep. George Orwell's observations, perceptions and experiences in the same region are the sparks igniting our ideas and rooting our proposal in a deeper past. What remains or resonates from this time and what has been erased?

Alan Pergusey
Alan Pergusey, a Leeds-based artist, is also interested in Orwell's view of Albion. Through paintings of marker buoys and mid-twentieth century coastal military defences he is exploring what it is to live on an island at the edge of a continent, and what ideas of patriotism and splendid isolation might actually mean in a post-Brexit climate. He writes:

> Orwell's analysis of the tensions between patriotism and nationalism implicit in 'The Lion and the Unicorn' and 'The English People' permeate these landscapes; isolated, defensive and faintly paranoid.

Nigel Pugh
A young Nigel Pugh first encountered the writing of Orwell whilst on a holiday with a new school friend's family. He writes:

> His mother suggested that he and I walk into the nearby town as a way of getting to know one another. It may have been

GLENN IBBITSON

that she was already sick of the sight of me and had thought this up as a ruse to get rid of me for the day. Whatever her motives, the result was spectacularly successful (from my point of view) with the result of returning a few hours later having established that her son couldn't drink more than half a bottle of QC sherry without losing the use of his legs. Unlike me, he had never tried alcohol before so it was something of a shock to a hardened drinker like myself to see the pitiful state into which he had fallen. I managed eventually to carry him home, but instead of being grateful (I could have easily forgotten him and left him behind) his mother banned me from going anywhere near him for the rest of the week, and confined me during daylight hours to a conservatory in which there was a shelf of books.

I selected one called *Animal Farm*. Once finished, an astonished 12-year-old hedonist became an astonished politically aware 12-year-old hedonist. From that moment onward my every delinquency became an action against the state … and always in Snowball's cause. The drawing provided is something that came to me almost as soon as the project was mentioned. Of all Orwell's writing *Homage to Catalonia* is my personal favourite. It encapsulates the glare of truth from which Orwell's gaze never flinched. The saddest part of the book is the account of the fighting between the various factions in Barcelona – a revolution eating itself alive.

My drawing is of a dead Anarchist. As you can probably tell from my introductory tale, the Anarchists were always going to be my favourites and thanks to Orwell, they still are.

Interestingly, Nigel became an aerial photographer for a freelance surveying company, which fed his own work with source material for many years and leads us conveniently to those artists whose submissions deal with surveillance issues in our society.

CONTRIBUTORS: SURVEILLANCE

Liam Ainscough
Liam Ainscough's installations comprise omnipresent surveillance drones over cityscapes; constantly monitoring the populace below. He writes:

The use of CCTV has, in recent years, been introduced under the guise of security but it comes at a price, as the UK becomes the most watched state in the world. According to a British Security Industry Authority (BSIA) report of July 2013, Britain has a CCTV camera for every 11 people. A staggering 5.9 million closed-circuit television cameras have been installed in the country since the 1980s. After 9/11 and the emerging threat to westerners from extremist groups, there has been a conscious effort by the controlling states to have surveillance less in the shadows and more on display; as an indicator of public security.

Simultaneously, there has also been the rapid development and implementation of technology enabling remote extermination, without battlefield risk or direct accountability. Drones are no longer the passive eye of reconnaissance. They are precision instruments of annihilation. As with the advent of any new technology, it takes time for it to become public knowledge especially if used in a covert manner. Through my research and practice I hope to lodge these concepts in the public domain.

It seemed apposite that Liam's drone should become the updated poster image of the current social media call for artist's submissions to 'Room 103'.

Garry Barker

Garry Barker's images arrive before the viewer as light-hearted cartoons; they gradually shape-shift into something stranger and faintly disquieting, and finally emerge as fully-fledged icons of unease. Always watching…. He writes:

> Orwell would no doubt have been truly mortified to find out that Cambridge Analytica were now engaged in the manipulation of the democratic process via data mining and psychological profiling, contributing to the development of sophisticated social control systems and buttressed by a fear-mongering media. Perhaps more worrying is the corrosion of language, so that words no longer mean what they used to mean. Politicians and big business can say one thing and mean another, they can define our realities.
>
> This dark period of our history will need its images and if they are the right ones perhaps they might help in a late rear-guard action, designed to remind the world of once-cherished ideals that are now being sold off in the media frenzy of late capitalism. These images are made in response to conversations held with others who are becoming more and more worried by the rise of a society that is shaped by capital and manipulated by media-constructed fear.

Dave Stephens

Dave Stephens is a sculptor, performance artist and film maker. He has offered up a short video. He writes:

> 'The Sky is Falling' describes an aerial attack on the last remaining outpost against conformism. It is a rough video draft of a more ambitious work in progress on the military capabilities of drone technology. I am collaborating with my son William on this

GLENN IBBITSON

project. He recently visited Berlin and met a Syrian refugee who was being refused entry to a club. Will was not able to persuade the doormen to let the Syrian in so instead they both headed to a refugees' club which proved far more interesting. The Syrian later sent Will a picture of a decimated town that had only one house left standing. He said that that was his house. The image that he sent became the focus of this collaboration.

This project is moving towards a more expansive film exploring the ways that surveillance is becoming an everyday part of our society. Very much like the Orwellian imagery in *Nineteen Eighty-Four*.

Dalton Desborough

Dalton Desborough has taken his experience of sculpting with latex from art college into the arena of commercial and medical prosthetics. He writes:

'EYE' is a sculpture that references the surveillance apparatus which saturates the London of both *Nineteen Eighty-Four* and 2018. Within the eyeball of the sculpture the pupil is made from a crystal clear resin that is backed with a concave mirror. The audience see themselves whilst observing the sculpture. This creates a tension; they are constantly being watched. Even if they are no longer looking at the sculpture, 'EYE' still looks over them. The use of silicone is used to help make the resemblance of the eye a human one; magnifying the effect that there is always someone watching; like a shadow that can't be shaken off…

Emma Saunders

Emma Saunders saw 'Room 103' as an opportunity to dust off a site-specific video/installation work protesting against the proposed imposition of Identity Cards on UK citizens. She writes:

In collaboration with the human rights organisation, Liberty, and its 'Say No To ID' campaign was a projection on to the Houses of Parliament. It ran for 25 minutes from midnight, 6 October2006. It was a strange experience. We had a van parked on Westminster Bridge for almost 30 minutes with the back open and a large projector shining at the Houses of Parliament. The lads operating it were dressed in black and some wore balaclavas – in all that time we experienced no police intervention – only two community officers who mentioned parking restrictions. Bear in mind this was just after a one mile protest exclusion zone had been imposed around Parliament Square. Shami Chakrabati, then Liberty director, and MPs were present during the screening; passers-by took photographs – but the event received no press coverage and nothing was reported online afterwards. I emailed the newspapers but no coverage resulted. Very odd. All I can think is that the Home Office had possibly intervened. It was, in some respects, a disappointing outcome, almost as if it had never happened. Fitting really.

CONTRIBUTORS: SUPPRESSION AND CONFORMITY

Clare Ferguson Walker

Clare Ferguson Walker, a painter, sculptor and forthright voice on the slam poetry and comedy circuits, takes as her theme Orwell's defence of individual rights to dissent, appropriating traditional images from Western art and transforming them with radical stylistic and representational modifications. 'The Ship of Fools' is a raft of proles, various aspects of flawed , individualistic, deviant and creative humanity cast adrift, to be replaced by conformists all too willing to accept smoothly operating, socially engineered worldviews without question.

'Clockwork Heart' makes this case at a more personal level. Something of a self-portrait, this is individual as automaton; a synecdoche for an entire people reduced to perfectly efficient but disposable components; readily replaceable pieces in a greater state mechanism. The resulting polychromatic ceramics are at once beautiful and pitiful.

Kath Wilkinson

Kath Wilkinson is a director of promotional films. She has worked in the corporate video sector as first model-maker then director for almost 20 years. A cineaste who looks to commercial cinema rather than art video, her work is usually seen only at 'pop-up' events – and by invitation only. She writes:

> For 'Room 103', I looked closely at the three commercial film versions of *Nineteen Eighty-Four*, and how they treated the climactic scene of Winston Smith's betrayal of Julia. In contrast to the black and white film versions of Rudolf Cartier (1954) and Michael Anderson (1956) and of the washed-out hues of the Michael Radford feature released in 1984, I wanted to make the fear visceral through saturated full colour within a fully illuminated room. Orwell knew that the expectation of torture was a psychologically more effective tool than the physical act itself. 'Do it to Julia – not Me' is four minutes of a head in tight crop; centred on the victim's mouth distorted by fear, head rocking to and fro in a vain attempt to avoid its impending fate. Because I used the rats' point of view, closing slowly in on the face, I elected to utilise that animal's faster metabolic rate and reactions, so the victim's movements and accompanying pleadings are correspondingly slowed down. The distorted screams are overlaid by a chattering redolent of rats' teeth to create a noisescape. The whole is jerkily edited like badly spliced

GLENN IBBITSON

and looped pieces of footage. A rough cut for an Oceania corporate video; a torturer's educational manual, or perhaps a public information broadcast *pour encourager les autres*...

Glenn ibbitson
The barcode is the symbol *nonpareil* of 21st Century commerce. It is projected across the model here to represent the subjugation of the individual to societal requirements. When humanity is depersonalised and assigned a particular value like any other product, set by market forces, how much easier it becomes for developed society to satisfy both its economic and sexual requirements. Here is humanity consumed with no more regard than any other expendable, off-the-shelf, imported/trafficked merchandise.

'Barcode: 6079 Smith, W' is something of a personal appeal against the constant erosion of self-worth, individualism and dignity. It serves as a warning that a state in which its citizens are treated as commodity and in which subjects are willingly bought off by diversionary, cheap products – in effect, by prolefood – risks disaster. The sub-title refers to a certain Winston Smith and the number assigned him by the Party.

'ROOM 103' @SAUL HAY GALLERY, MANCHESTER
The Barcode painting was selected as an exhibit by the organisers of the Newlight Art Prize at Bowes Museum last autumn. It was here that I met gallery owners Catherine and Ian Hay. I had seen them looking at the work, and its obscure title allowed me to introduce myself with an explanation. As with so many conversations over the last couple of years, this one turned from the exhibition on view to the subject of Orwell's journalism and its influence on contemporary thought and culture. The possibility of collaborating on a themed exhibition was left hanging in the air as we exchanged email addresses and goodbyes.

On 24 February 2018, Ian messaged me inviting me to visit the gallery to discuss a showing of work comprising a selection from 'Room 103'. The Saul Hay Gallery is a fairly new addition to the Manchester arts map, so it was only as I approached the premises that I realised just how significant a location this would be for a tribute to Orwell. On one side of the gallery is the terminus basin of the Bridgewater Canal, one of the early fuses which ignited the industrial revolution. On the other, a viaduct which carried the world's first passenger railway from Manchester to Liverpool; confirming the development of urbanisation. The problems arising from both these related phenomena provided George Orwell with the material for his lifetime of writing and study.

Railway Cottage is a handsome Victorian red brick building of the type Orwell would have been familiar with as he filled notebooks with observations on the way to Wigan, though the accumulation of half a century's industrial grime may have masked their simple elegance from him at that time. (As a child growing up in Leeds through the 1960s, I thought my city's town hall had been built from an unspecified black stone. Only when the municipal buildings in this part of West Yorkshire were cleaned in the eighties did their architectural details re-emerge in all their full Victorian glory.) High on the front wall of Railway Cottage is a clock-face. It doesn't strike thirteen, but I think Orwell might be tickled by the notion that at this venue, the time is always six minutes before six…

Catherine and Ian have been a delight to liaise with and have been proactive in organising the show well in advance of the actual event. Dates were finalised for an exhibition due to run from 11 October to 11 November 2018. It was hoped that Richard Blair, Patron of The Orwell Society, would be available to open proceedings at the preview which was due to take place on Thursday 11 October. This has fulfilled my hopes for the project earlier than expected, but is only the first of what I hope will be many gallery venues. The blog remains operational for further business, so if you would like to contribute work, or know of any artists who would like to submit pieces in response to any of the myriad threads running through Orwell's *oeuvre* do please visit the online gallery homepage which lays out the submission procedure.

- Adapted and updated from a presentation delivered as part of the Third George Orwell Studies Conference, Goldsmiths, University of London. 30 May 2018. All the contributors' artworks can be viewed on their own named page at orwellroom103.wordpress.com.

REFERENCES

Baker, A. (2015) *Homage to Homage to Catalonia* (self-produced). Available online at https://issuu.com/tonybaker2/docs/homage_to_homage__digital

Steffan Jones, P. (2013) *The Trigger-Happiness*, Clunderwen, United Kingdom: Starborn Books

WEBSITES

Baldry, K.: https://vimeo.com/228541866

British Security Industry Association: https://www.bsia.co.uk/Portals/4/Publications/302-bsia-overview.pdf

Liberty: https://www.libertyhumanrights.org.uk

Newlight Art Prize: http://newlight-art.org.uk/prize-exhibition/

Saul Hay Gallery: https://www.saulhayfineart.co.uk

Stephens, D.: http://wwwdavestephens.blogspot.co.uk/2015/09/syria-film-sky-is-falling.html

GLENN IBBITSON

NOTE ON THE CONTRIBUTOR

Glenn Ibbitson is a fine artist and curator whose artwork is generated from activity across the waveband of visual disciplines, from drawing and painting to narrative video and book art. Following a career as a scenic artist for the BBC and later, the wider film and television industry, he relocated to West Wales to paint full-time. His art has been compared to a self-assembly furniture kit – don't expect to find all the components or an instruction manual in the box. In spite of this, his work has been shown in London, New York, Tokyo and Rio de Janeiro and is housed in private and public collections across six continents.

Orwell and the Appeal of Opium

DARCY MOORE

Gordon Bowker posited, in his biography of George Orwell, that 'opium never appealed to Blair' (Bowker 2003: 82). However, circumstantial evidence, some of it uncovered post-publication, suggests it is possible Orwell smoked opium in Burma. This paper also argues that this is all the more likely given his father's lifelong involvement in the British opium industry in India.

Keywords: Eric Arthur Blair, Burma, Orwell, Richard Walmsley Blair, Captain H. R. Robinson, Henry Osborne, opium, drug

> 'People always grow up like their names. It took me nearly thirty years to work off the effects of being called Eric.'
> Letter to Rayner Heppenstall, 16 April 1940

> '…to find that George Orwell was Eric A. Blair, as I say, was rather like seeing a flying saucer arrive at your front door…'
> Roger Beadon, 1969 interview

> 'There was a cool sweetish smell of opium.'
> *Burmese Days* (1934)

George Orwell (1903-1950), born Eric Arthur Blair, was the son of an opium dealer. His father, Richard Walmsley Blair (1857-1939), was a sub-deputy agent in the Opium Department of the Indian Civil Service and Orwell spent the first year of life on the sub-continent. His father, for the best part of four decades, served the British Empire, working his way slowly through the ranks of the civil service, legally peddling opium, before retiring to the upmarket, thoroughly respectable seaside town of Southwold, back in England.

Eric Blair suggested the pseudonym George Orwell to his publisher for his first book, *Down and Out in Paris and London* (1933), largely to avoid embarrassing his father (Wadhams 1984: 45). We have no record of Orwell being embarrassed nor concerned by his father's line of work. The Old Etonian, after serving five years in Burma with the Indian Imperial Police (1922-1927), knew all about the 'dirty work of empire' and there was none dirtier than the opium trade.

DARCY MOORE Orwell never explicitly wrote about the opium trade, most likely out of deference to his father. But circumstantial evidence, explored in this paper, suggests he personally experimented with the drug when he was a police officer in Burma. He was always a secretive man, skilfully maintaining his privacy and effectively segregating friends. He insisted no biography be written after his death.

Orwell's experience of illicit drugs is understandably challenging to document with indisputable evidence. We do know from his diaries that he smoked marijuana in Morocco (Davison 2010: 106) and wrote about opium in *Burmese Days* (*CWGO* II 1997 [1934]: 132-133). In *Down and Out in Paris and London*, he explored a cocaine deal gone wrong (*CWGO* I 1997 [1933]: 124-126) and *Nineteen Eighty-Four* makes extensive reference to the use of drugs in a dystopian society (Orwell 1949: 173, 195, 280). Is it reasonable to assume that Orwell based most of his reportage and fiction on lived experience?

Rules never much concerned Orwell. One of the few photographs we have of him is as a teenager, insouciantly smoking, a hand-rolled cigarette hanging from his mouth (Crick 1992 [1980]: 382). Eton prohibited such activity but Orwell had a penchant, even though it was 'awfully hard to get', for Turkish tobacco in his teens (*CWGO* X 1998: 79). Smoking was to become a life-long habit. As an adult, Orwell chain-smoked a pungent, black, shag tobacco – rather than the more exotic, expensive cigarettes preferred by his peers – until his early death from tuberculosis (and probably over-smoking, too) in 1950 (Shelden 1997: 282).

ORWELL'S BURMESE DAYS

In December 1922, a year after he graduated from Eton, Eric Blair arrived in Rangoon to commence his career as a Probationary Assistant Superintendent Police Officer. What happened, professionally and personally, during those five years in Burma to the young man who had previously led such a sheltered existence? There are few primary sources that survive but some significant signposts complement what we learn from his novel, *Burmese Days*, first published in the USA amid concerns about libel (*CWGO* II 1997 [1934]: 309).

Two of his most brilliantly disturbing essays, 'Shooting an Elephant' (*CWGO* X 1998: 501-506) and 'A Hanging' (ibid: 207-210) stem from his experiences in Burma. We have a small number of important but frustratingly superficial firsthand reports from people – in particular, Roger Beadon, George Stuart and Christopher Hollis – who knew Orwell in Burma. There are the official government records and reports, crime statistics as well as several genuinely fascinating memoirs, including unpublished manuscripts, from police officers who served contemporaneously with him in the

1920s. Most of his letters have not survived, although a new cache, written to his lover Eleanor Jaques, has recently been publicised. He describes the weirdness of the Burmese landscape and the effect it had on his consciousness to her. The bundle – found stashed and marked, 'letters to be destroyed' – is still unpublished as this paper goes to print (Taylor 2018).

The impact of the five years in Burma may be discerned by comparing a photograph taken in 1921 (Meyers 2000: 152), as his Eton days drew to a close, with Orwell's 1927 passport picture where he sports what most would describe as a 'Hitler moustache' (National Archives, MEPO 38/69). His cherubic visage has been replaced by a harder, more knowing one. We are looking at a very different person. This is a man whose experiences have changed him irrevocably and, as his family soon discovered when he returned to Southwold, is no longer prepared to follow the expected path.

SOUTHWOLD AND THE OPIUM DEPARTMENT

When Orwell returns home to Southwold on leave, in August 1927, he has to tell his father that he is resigning, not just from his job but from a lifestyle. Sons born into Anglo-Indian families rarely turned their back on a tradition that ensured financial stability, status and respectability (Bowker 2003: 11).

The elder Blair (1857-1939) spent thirty-seven years in India. His son lasted just five in Burma. He was throwing away a good income and a pension. One imagines the awkwardness of the conversation for Orwell, while holidaying in Cornwall, explaining this life-changing decision (Bowker 2003: 98). One thing is almost certain: he would not have criticised his father's time peddling opium for the British empire. *I want to be a writer* rather than, *I find the whole business of being a police officer too 'beastly'* – one of his favourite adjectives and the first word he ever uttered (ibid: 15) seems most likely. Father was never going to be pleased.

R. W. Blair was employed in the Indian Civil Service regulating the quality, production, collection and transportation of opium from 1875 until his retirement in 1912. Eric, his second child and only son, was born in Motihari, Bihar, a small Indian town near the Nepalese border where his father was stationed in 1903. The three-room bungalow where Blair lived with his much younger wife, Ida Mabel Limouzin (1875-1942), and eldest daughter Marjorie (1898-1946), was conveniently located near a large warehouse used for storing opium that would later be processed and exported to China (Rahman 2014). Jeffrey Meyers, one of Orwell's biographers, explains Blair's role in this controversial government opium franchise:

> A sub-deputy's job was to supervise the poppy growers in his district and make sure the crop was cultivated in the most efficient

way. The government itself made cash advances to cultivators, purchased their product, carried on the manufacturing process and made the final sale of the poppy juice to the factories and exporters in Patna and Calcutta. The opium revenue, next to that from land and salt, was the largest single increment to the Indian treasury and generated sixteen percent of its total income. As long as the money came pouring in, neither the Opium Department nor the Indian Government was greatly concerned about what happened to the tons of opium (illegal in India) that reached the dope fiends in China. In fact, the British quite deliberately used the drug to weaken and undermine the fragile structure of the doomed Chinese Empire, which had fought and lost two opium wars with Britain in the mid-nineteenth century and finally collapsed in 1912 (Meyers 2000: 5).

Opium and empire 'marched together' and a financial dependence grew on the drug, as analysis of the revenue data between 1790-1934 reveals (Deming 2011: 5). Opium, never intended for British domestic consumption, had immense strategic importance for the triangular trade between China, Britain and India as it became increasingly essential to offset trade deficits, especially for silver (ibid: 10-11).

Orwell never wrote about his father and it is difficult to know to what extent, if at all, he discussed the opium trade, so fundamental to balancing the British Empire's books, with him. Biographers have very little to analyse where this father-son relationship is concerned. Considering Orwell's predilection for 'seeing things as they truly are', one imagines they must have discussed the work he did for all those years in India. Similarly, his mother, who must have been aware of the controversy that surrounded the trade, surely had conversations with her intelligent son about his father's work. There is some considerable evidence, however, that this might not have been the case.

In 1983, Stephen Wadhams interviewed dozens of people who knew Orwell. Few could speak with any authority about his family or early life. Mabel Fierz, who first knew him in Southwold, after he had resigned from the police, felt he greatly loved and respected his parents, especially his father. She emphasises that he would never wish to embarrass them – but, by quitting his job in Burma and tramping with the down-and-outs to gather material for his first book, had done so (Wadhams 1984: 44-45).

Dennis Collings and Orwell were 'best friends' and spent much time together in Southwold in the periods immediately after Burma and Paris (ibid: 35). They were unusual young men in the context of this very conservative town. Collings was interviewed several times, providing particularly valuable insights into Orwell's 'rather silent' relationship with his father saying, 'there was not a lot of talk' (Coppard 1984: 78). Collings sympathised with the elder Blair's point of view that his son had 'gone off the rails' (ibid: 80) and explains:

> Father you see didn't like the idea of him having given up his job in Burma and father thought he should have been making a name for himself in the Burmese service and you know there would be a pension ahead of him and all that kind of thing. That was the main cause of contention, they never had rows about it or anything of that kind but there was this feeling that he was wasting ... (Wadhams 1983: unpublished recording).

Even though he did not wish to embarrass his parents, in *Burmese Days*, written mostly at the family home in Southwold, Orwell mockingly satirises his father's lifestyle describing 'Anglo-Indians littered about in all stages of decomposition, all talking and talking about what happened in Boggleywalah in '88! Poor devils...' (*CWGO* II 1997 [1934]: 72). In *The Road to Wigan Pier* (1937), Orwell says, after his five years in the Indian Police: 'I hated the imperialism I was serving with a bitterness which I probably cannot make clear' (*CWGO* V 1997 [1937]: 134). The presence of an unemployed son, residing at the family home with such attitudes, must have been a source of tension for his parents.

The unconventional, failed, Orwell provided a rich source of gossip around Southwold, and not just for quitting his job (Binns 2018: 57). As ever, unconcerned by rules, Orwell had developed a liking for married women in Burma (Bowker 2003: 88). Mabel Fierz, herself married when she met Orwell, described him as a 'womaniser' and there is some suggestion she had an affair with the younger man (ibid: 130). Fierz had intimate knowledge of Orwell's romantic pursuits, including a failed liaison in Paris with a woman he intended to marry, who stole his possessions (Wadhams 1984: 45). There is no evidence at all that this woman was drug-addicted, but in the bohemian quarter Orwell resided this would not have been uncommon (Boon 2002: 71-73).

Collings' wife, Eleanor Jaques, maintained a correspondence with Orwell for many years, including (as yet unpublished) letters from Burma. The nature of their relationship can be deduced as the bundle was marked 'to be destroyed' (Taylor: 2018). *A Clergyman's Daughter* (1935) satirises gossip, in a mocking tone, with a dismissive, 'in a town which *everyone* is either a bigamist, a pederast or a drug-taker, the worst scandal loses its sting' (*CWGO* III 1997 [1935]: 46). Orwell hid much from his parents about his personal life but how much did his father hide from him?

DARCY MOORE Orwell's father was not a reader, diarist or much of a letter-writer. However, there is evidence of what life was like in the Opium Department, in the shape of twenty-six handwritten diaries, bound in original cloth, with several thousand pages of entries written legibly in ink, giving an authentic insight into the practical, challenging nature of the elder Blair's work. The diarist, Henry Osborne (1840-1905) served contemporaneously with Blair, in the Opium Department, India Office, of the British Government in Bengal.[1]

Osborne's diaries detail the day-to-day life, work and subsequent retirement of a sub-deputy opium agent during the period 1876-1905. The oldest – written in *Pettitt's Octavo Diary* – was a little worn being more than 140 years old. Osborne's other 25 diaries are in magnificent, near fine condition (surprisingly considering the nature of his work 'marching' from one village to another in the dust and heat). Most of his days in Bengal are recorded using *Letts's Diary or Bills Due Book and Almanac* and when he retired, *T, J. & J. Smith's Post Diary with an Almanack*.

Osborne's career as a colonial official began in April 1865 but the diaries for the first decade of his employment either never existed or are lost. He was first-employed as a 5th Grade Sub-Deputy Opium Agent stationed at Ghazeepore (Ghazipur). Blair's career, from the age of eighteen in 1875, commenced at the same lowly rank. It is noteworthy that Osborne's father was also employed in the same role. Orwell's decision to quit the Burmese Police was genuinely unusual for someone born into an Anglo-Indian family.

Did the elder Blair regale his son with stories about opium and India? Osborne and Blair are government sanctioned drug-dealers. Such a profession has obvious risks and would provide good anecdotes, if Orwell's father had talked to his son about his work. For example, Osborne slept with a 'derringer' living in fear of intruders entering his tent at night:

> Loaded derringer & fired a couple of shots in the evening – reloaded and placed it under the mattress of our bed at night (Osborne: 18 February 1877).

Managing the cultivation and distribution of the British Empire's opium trade was always going to be a challenging business and Osborne records conflict with his boss, 'the Agent' (Osborne: 17 September 1877).

The Registers of Employees of the East India Company and the India Office reveal that Blair and Osborne's superior, the 'Opium Agent' for Benares and the most senior official in the Opium Department, was J. H. Rivett-Carnac (1838-1923). He gave evidence to the *First*

Report of the Royal Commission on Opium in 1894 (Rowntree 1895) and is an excellent primary source for understanding the information in Osborne's diaries. His obituary provides useful insight into both the man and official:

> In accordance with the family tradition of the Rivetts he spent most of his life in India, where he had a very distinguished career, in both civil and military capacities. In addition to his public life in the Indian Civil Service, he had many private hobbies of a more purely intellectual nature, in any of which he would have obtained eminence had it held his somewhat over-versatile attention for longer than a few years at a time (*The Spectator*: 5 May 1923).

Rivett-Carnac wrote about his life and times as well as his intellectual hobbies, including archaeology, publishing *Prehistoric Remains in Central India*. His memoirs, *Many Memories of Life in India, at Home, and Abroad*, published in 1910, two years before Blair retired, provides insight into the work and lives of men as they progressed through the ranks of the Opium Department. Rivett-Carnac acknowledges 'the overworked district officials' and the following, lengthy quotation, provides context for many of Osborne's diary entries and Richard Blair's long career in the field:

> … the Indian Government draw from opium a revenue of about four million sterling. As to the merits of this source of revenue it is not my intention to enlarge. A Commission was sent out to India in 1893 to examine the whole question, and in their report will be found all the information that the most exacting inquirer can demand. The chief sources of supply were, and still are, the Behar districts of Bengal, and the southern and eastern districts of the North-Western, now termed the United Provinces. Under the Act pertaining to the subject, no one could grow the poppy plant without a licence from Government. And all the produce of the plant so grown had to be delivered over to the Government officials in the poppy-growing districts at a fixed rate. The opium so collected was then despatched to the Government factories, where it was packed and thence sent down to Calcutta. These chests of opium were there sold by auction, and the difference between the price thus obtained and the cost of the drug, and of the establishment of the Opium Department, represented the opium revenue (Rivett-Carnac 1910: 304-305).

He continues to say that the establishments necessary for the working of the department were presided over by two so-called agents, one with his headquarters at Patna, where there was a factory, the other at Ghazipur, where a second factory was situated. Each agent had under him a considerable staff of Europeans and natives: generally a European officer, with sometimes a European assistant, in each of the districts where opium was cultivated. This officer had to select the lands on which the plant was to be grown and issue to each cultivator a licence in approved form. When collected, the drug was brought to the headquarters of this officer who weighed it and paid for it according to certain rules. It was then sent down by rail or boat to Ghazipur. Rivett-Carnac continues:

> The processes at the factory were confined to seeing that the drug was of a uniform consistence as regards the moisture therein contained, and to making it into balls, like large cannon-shot, of which the covering was formed by the flower petals of the plant. For the duties of granting licences, inspecting and measuring the lands, seeing that none without licence were sown, for receiving, weighing, paying, &c, and for despatching the drug to the factory, the European officer had a considerable Native staff…and a large number of men employed in the districts to supervise cultivation, prevent illicit cultivation, smuggling…and that what with this and the many other questions connected with a large Department and a great revenue, his hands could be pretty full (ibid: 305-306).

Orwell's father is often mentioned, in biographies of his literary son, as having very slow career progression. Rivett-Carnac tells us that:

> Promotion was slow, and prospects were not good. Still a man could rise eventually to a salary of £1200 a-year, with a pension on retirement of £500-a-year. A young man so started was provided for, in a way, for life, and there were many who could not resist the temptation of thus disposing of a son, and relieving themselves of the expense and anxiety of further education. So there was a considerable demand on my miserable patronage, and having fortunately no poor relations to provide for, I did my best, whilst trying to secure a good class of youth for the work, to assist deserving old officers who were known to have large families and proportionate difficulties to struggle with (ibid: 307).

There is a 'M Rivett-Carnac' listed as serving the Opium Department in 1878. Rivett-Carnac had no children so one assumes this must be a relative he was assisting by his patronage.

Rivett-Carnac made no value judgement on the 'merits' of the opium trade but tucked away at the back of Osborne's 1876 diary is a very unexpected address in London. One can only guess why Osborne had listed the 'Anglo-Oriental Society for the Suppression of the Opium Trade – Canada Building, King St. Westminster SW'. The society had only been formed by Quaker businessmen in 1874 and was conveniently located near the India Office and Houses of Parliament (Inglis 2018: 235-236). One would imagine his employer, the British government, or more specifically, the Opium Department of the India Office, would hardly be enamoured of this interest. Did Osborne visit the office? Did he provide information? It is a fascinating prospect to think that this particular sub-deputy opium agent (third class in 1876-1877) had a social conscience. There is no evidence that Richard Blair had qualms about the production of this drug which had such a lengthy history of consumption in India.

When the produce of the opium poppy (papaver somniferum) was first consumed in India is uncertain. There is no hard evidence but is generally believed Alexander the Great (356-323 BCE) introduced it to India incidentally through trade (Inglis 2018: 20). During the Mughal Empire (1526-1707) poppy cultivation became a staple crop and opium sales a state monopoly by the late 16th century (Chopra 1955: 1-2). The Mughal emperors had a conspicuous culture of opium consumption at court resulting in significant ramifications for their rule (Honchell 2010: 6). Opium was embedded in Indian culture well before the arrival of British imperialism or the Opium Department R. W. Blair served.

ORWELL'S TATTOOS

Since the last major biographies were published, on the centenary of Orwell's birth, in 2003, it has been uncovered that Orwell had tattoos. In 2007, it was revealed that Britain's domestic intelligence agency MI5 and the Metropolitan Police Special Branch had Orwell under surveillance as a suspected communist sympathiser. This began in 1929 when he was residing in Paris after resigning from the Burmese Police (National Archives, MEPO 38/69). Orwell's passport details were in these newly released secret police files. His 1936 passport application describes him as 6ft 2 1/2 inches, with grey eyes, brown hair but most interestingly records 'tattoo marks on the backs of hands' in the 'visible distinguishing marks or peculiarities' section of the form (National Archives, MEPO 38/69). The 1927 passport photograph tells a story of Orwell's five years in Burma, as do his knuckles.

What does this information tell us about the former police officer turned journalist? Why did he get tattooed? Surely this was unusual for an Old Etonian and police officer? What did his parents and sisters think? Adrian Fierz, the son of Mabel Fierz who helped Orwell find a publisher for his first book, described these tattoos to Gordon Bowker as 'blue spots the shape of small grapefruits – one on each knuckle' (Bowker 2007). Fierz, who idolised Orwell, remembered them clearly during a telephone conversation with Bowker, saying he had been fascinated by such unusual markings as a boy.

These tattoos were apparently never mentioned by friends, girlfriends, wives or acquaintances to biographers. His son, Richard Blair, admittedly very young when Orwell died, does not remember them either (in conversation with me on Jura in June this year). They are not evident (although the reproduction quality is low) in Vernon Richards' photographs, shot at Orwell's Canonbury Square residence, in 1946 (1998) or in the portrait taken by Felix H. Man around the same time (1984 [1983]). They may have faded.

The MI5 and Special Branch files are unique sources for understanding Orwell from an official, government perspective. A secret report from 11 March 1936 reveals good insight into his resignation from the Burmese Police saying: 'Blair gave no official reason for terminating his appointment, but he is reported to have told his intimate friends that he could not bring himself to arrest persons for committing acts he did not think were wrong' (National Archives, MEPO 38/69). Another secret document from the same file dated 20 January 1942 notes that Orwell 'dresses in a bohemian fashion both at his office and in his leisure hours' (ibid). This was not the trajectory that his dapper, conservative father would have imagined when he agreed to fund his son's police uniforms back in 1922 (E. A. Blair's recruitment file).

One reading of his life posits that Blair reinvents himself as Orwell, the literary man seeking truth, from the publication of *Down and Out in Paris and London*. This may have been partly due to his indiscretions and misdemeanours as a police officer and man. 'St George' he is not but certainly Orwell constructed an identity as a man of letters who was more secular than saint and more trenchant, and clear-eyed, than any of his generation. Some claim 'Orwell' is his most successfully realised character (Williams 1974: 52).

Burma was the beginning of this transformation of Blair into Orwell (Stansky and Abrahams 1972, 1980). The conventional view is that his experiences of crime, responsibility at a young age and the awful nature of doing the 'dirty work of empire' led him to find his true nature which he had denied for too long. He was to become a 'famous writer' or fail in the attempt (Wadhams 1984: 13). Perhaps there is more to this transformation. Who influenced the young Blair in Burma? How did he spend his off-duty time?

We know that Orwell could speak 'high-flown Burmese' with the Buddhist priests in the temples he visited (Coppard 1984: 63). George Stuart, a friend who worked on the railways and knew Blair in Mandalay and Katha, claims the cash-strapped young police officer was encouraged by the thousand-rupee bonus each time he passed a language test (Stuart: Orwell Archive). Curiosity almost certainly led him to explore widely around Mandalay where he likely explored market-stalls in the bazaar, brothels and opium dens (Bowker 2003: 81).

A MODERN DE QUINCEY

There is evidence that Orwell was more than just a passing acquaintance of Captain Herbert Reginald Robinson (1896-1965) and that this friendship perhaps offers clues about Orwell's relationship with opium. Robinson, born in London, served in the Indian Army and Burmese Military Police from 1915 until his retirement in 1923 (*London Gazette*, 30 May 1924). Described as the 'most disreputable man in Burma' (Shelden 1991: 97), there is no evidence he was 'cashiered', as some biographers have written (Stansky and Abrahams 1972: 117). However, in 1925, opium-addicted and fearing imprisonment for debt, he attempted suicide in Mandalay, blinding himself permanently (Robinson 1942: 143).

Peter Davison established that Orwell was in Mandalay – for a year from November 1922 and then again from mid-December 1923 to late January 1924 – when Robinson was resident (*CWGO* XIV 1998: 35). Significantly, Orwell reviewed Robinson's memoir, *A Modern De Quincey – An Autobiography*, on publication, in 1942, for the *Observer*. What was the nature of their relationship? Orwell spent limited time 'at the club' with colleagues drinking and could not have spent all his time friendless, reading in his room (Coppard 1984: 62).

Gerry Abbott convincingly theorises that 'the Poet', in Robinson's memoir, is Eric Blair (Abbott 2006: 44-47) although this has been challenged (Baker 2018: unpublished). If Abbott is correct, Orwell was with Robinson the night he first smoked opium:

> One evening, towards the end of April, I was sitting in the Upper Burma Club discussing my plan with two friends, whom I will call the Poet and the Padre. As conversation lagged and there seemed to be nothing to do, the Poet suggested we should go down to the bazaar and have something to eat at a Chinese restaurant (Robinson 1942: 60).

Abbott rightly questions why Robinson did not identify either the 'Poet' or 'Padre' two decades after the events described in his memoir (Robinson 2004: xiii). The book contract, signed by Robinson in 1941, records the original title as *Burma Road* (Harrap and Co. 1941). Why did the publisher change the title? Robinson resided at Burma Road as an infant making it a sensible title for his memoir. Is it possible draft manuscripts may have had the title and names changed, on legal advice, to the eponymous 'Poet' and 'Padre'? Robinson or the publisher may not have wanted the author of *Burmese Days* to be identified. This is, although admittedly speculative, an area for further research.

It is important to realise that Orwell reviewed *A Modern De Quincey* while employed by the BBC (1941-1943). Perhaps Robinson, mindful of Orwell's position, chose to protect his reputation? If Orwell had smoked opium with Robinson or elsewhere, it was hardly something to be mentioned in his book review. It may be a mark of his relationship from 'the old days' that he even reviewed such a minor book at all, especially if, as Gerry Abbott suggests, Orwell is 'the Poet'. Orwell was certainly fond of Robinson:

> Those who knew Captain Robinson in the old days will be glad to receive this evidence of his continued existence, and to see the photograph of him at the beginning of the book, completely cured of the opium habit and apparently well-adjusted and happy, in spite of his blindness (*CWGO* XIV 1998: 34-35).

Bowker, understandably, based his 'opium never appealed to Blair' judgement on the strength of Orwell's comment in the review that:

> Those who knew the author in Mandalay in 1923 were completely unable to understand why a young, healthy and apparently happy man should give himself up to such a debilitating and – in a European – unusual vice, and on this point the book throws no further light. Captain Robinson merely explains that one night in Mandalay he happened to see some Chinese smoking their opium, decided to try what it was like, and thereafter became a habitual opium-smoker (ibid: 34).

However, in the same review, Orwell's observations, especially that the pleasures of the drug are 'indescribable', may be read as evidence of both personal, along with policing, experience:

> What are the pleasures of opium? Like other pleasures, they are, unfortunately, indescribable. It is easier to describe the miseries which the smoker suffers when deprived of his drug; he is seized with feverish restlessness, then with violent fits of yawning, and finally howls like a dog, a noise so distressing that when an opium-smoker is imprisoned in an Indian jail he is usually, quite illegally, given diminishing doses to keep him quiet (ibid: 34).

The following, lengthy passage from *Burmese Days*, also displays a knowledge of opium that may have come from policing except it is notable that the protagonist, Flory, is 'a friend' of Li Yeik:

> They went into the shop, which seemed dark after the outer air. Li Yeik, who was sitting smoking among his baskets of merchandise – there was no counter – hobbled eagerly forward when he saw who had come in. Flory was a friend of his. He was an old bent-kneed man dressed in blue, wearing a pigtail, with a chinless yellow face, all cheekbones, like a benevolent skull. He greeted Flory with nasal honking noises which he intended for Burmese, and at once hobbled to the back of the shop to

call for refreshments. There was a cool sweetish smell of opium. Long strips of red paper with black lettering were pasted on the walls, and at one side there was a little altar with a portrait of two large, serene-looking people in embroidered robes, and two sticks of incense smouldering in front of it (*CWGO* II 1997 [1934]: 132-133).

Robinson, described as a 'pioneer hippie drop-out' (Crick 1992 [1980]: 154), had a smoking den in his own home, screened by 'deep red velvet curtains, some nine feet in height ... with everything an opium-smoker could desire' (Robinson 1942: 93-94). Orwell did not need to go to Chinatown or elsewhere to smoke the drug with his friend.

TATTOOS (AGAIN), ANIMALS AND POLICING

How much time did Orwell and Robinson spend together? They shared unusual interests; for example, both lived happily with the close company of animals. Robinson kept a menagerie, including a bear and blind monkey, along with ducks, hens and pigeons (Robinson 1942: 25-26). We know that Orwell was 'very fond of animals' including 'strays' (Stuart, Orwell Archive). Beadon, who trained with Blair in Mandalay, describes Orwell's living arrangements in particularly disparaging terms:

> I went there and as far as I can remember he had goats, geese, ducks and all sorts of things floating about downstairs, whereas I'd kept rather a nice house. It rather shattered me, but ... it didn't worry him what the house looked like... (Coppard 1984: 64-65).

Did Orwell accompany Robinson to Buddhist temples? One photograph of Robinson, in the robes of a monk, suggests that Orwell would have learnt a great deal from the older man who was first in Burma during 1915 (Robinson 1942: 14). If Blair conversed fluently with priests during his spare time it would seem likely that he explored temples with Robinson (Coppard 1984: 63).

Did Robinson also influence the superstitious Orwell to get tattooed? Tattooing at this time was a 'slowly dying custom' in Burma but one could still see men 'tattooed from waist to knee in complicated patterns so close together' that they appeared to be 'wearing dark indigo blue trunks' (Meer-Nemo 1969: 39). Robinson was heavily tattooed as a 'charm against death from a bullet-wound or the thrust of a knife' (Robinson 1942: 101). In a macabre sense, it worked! Even though attempting suicide, he was not killed. Robinson describes the 'painful' tattooing process at some length:

DARCY MOORE

...the upper part of my body was bare. He then proceeded, with very crude instruments, to inscribe or tattoo certain signs on my body. On my wrists he tattooed three circles; on the points of my shoulders three circles, with their centre dots; on my upper arms he tattooed the figure of a cock, one leg raised, made from the Burmese figures for one to ten; on my chest he tattooed a rough sketch of a pagoda; on the back of my neck three more circles, and on the top of my head something which I could not fathom but which I guessed to be some more circles. The instruments were very primitive, and the process was very painful (ibid: 101-102).

One assumes that Robinson took opium before undergoing the procedure but did Orwell when he was tattooed? There are detailed rules in the official manuals regarding policing opium in Burma (which fall outside the scope of this paper) and who could be registered for legal, government opium. It was legal for registered tattooists to dispense opium to their clients. The police form, 'Licence for the Possession of Defined Opium by a Tattooer for Tattooing Purposes', in the *The Burma Opium Manual, 1925,* indicates no more than 'five tolas in weight' of opium are to be possessed for this purpose (1927: 88). Theoretically, then, it was legal for Orwell to use opium while being tattooed.

Roger Franklin, writing as A. Meer-Nemo, in an unpublished manuscript, is a rich source for the realities of policing in Burma during the 1920s (Meer-Nemo 1969). He notes it was contrary to Buddhist teaching for the Burmese to smoke opium, and comparatively few did. He mentions that those most commonly being addicted were often engaged working logging in jungle areas (both Robinson and Orwell were based in Katha, a logging settlement and the thinly-disguised setting for *Burmese Days*). He explains that opium was obtainable from the government opium shops once the applicant had satisfied the 'Superintendent of Excise' that he was a licensed, habitual smoker. The main test of addiction was if the user could effectively manipulate the opium roasting pin. Franklin points out that 'no Burman would wish to proclaim himself a habitual smoker by taking out a licence and going to the Government opium-shop if he could avoid it, there were those who prepared to make a living by selling it to him at home' (Meer-Nemo 1969: 180).

Franklin was certainly not above what could be called 'drug tourism'. As the 'Superintendent in charge of Central Division, Rangoon City' (1923-1925), he arranges for some nurses to experience the seamier side of the city by organising a fake opium den:

To satisfy their curiosity, it was my custom to phone the proprietor of a certain Chinese hotel, saying 'dinner for four, and opium-den', on which he would suitably prepare one of the hotel rooms in a tasteful manner, and would arrange for a respectable, picturesquely clad, and benign-looking old gentleman to be in attendance. When the time came, he would greet us, and, after climbing on to the bed, his little grand-daughter would prepare and hand him his pipe, he would start to smoke it, and we would then withdraw (Meer-Nemo 1969: 181-182).

The power of a police officer during the period Orwell was serving in Burma is particularly evident in an anecdote from Franklin about cocaine, where he explains to the nurses how impossible it is to stop the trade in narcotics. Franklin insists that the hotel proprietor procure the drug from the streets:

> …he gazed blankly at me and replied that he knew nothing about cocaine. However, when I repeated that I very much wanted these things and suggested that men should be sent out to try to find them, adding that there was nothing to fear if they were brought, and that no questions would be asked… (Meer-Nemo 1969: 182-183).

The proprietor does as requested and brings in a plate…

> … on which was a tiny folded slip of paper containing some cocaine, and a home-made hypodermic syringe. This consisted of a piece of glass tube drawn to a fine, sharp point, in which ran a plunger of cotton-wool on a thin cane rod, closed at the top with red sealing wax, through which the rod slid (ibid: 182-183).

These anecdotes establish the context in which Orwell, as a young police officer, in his early twenties, worked. He was in a powerful position with relatively low levels of supervision.

CONCLUSION

Often, facts about Orwell's life seem at odds with the author introduced to students by generations of English teachers at high school. Orwell covered his tracks well writing surprisingly little about his own life in the more than two million words published since his first professional piece – on censorship – appeared in a French newspaper in 1928. This guarded, intensely private person, even with his closest friends, is still a mystery. However, each year seems to turn up something that sheds new light on the man and his experiences.

Orwell has more lost years than Shakespeare. Considering the scholarly effort focused on uncovering his life and character there's little evidence, after graduating from Eton in 1921, about his time in Burma, Paris and in Southwold (on his resignation from the Burmese police). There is evidence that in the months before Blair left England for Burma, there was a botched seduction or attempted sexual assault of his childhood friend, Jacintha Buddicom, in September 1921 (Buddicom 2006 [1974]: 182).

DARCY MOORE

On his return in 1927, after five-years of service as a police officer, he intended to propose to Jacintha. She would not see him. Orwell was never to know that Jacintha was avoiding him as she was pregnant and later adopted the child (ibid: 183). This apparent rejection was a seminal moment in the life of the writer and propelled him further along the unusual path he was to travel during the next decade and more.

Orwell, on his death, was eulogised as the 'wintry conscience of a generation … a kind of saint' (Meyers 2010: 312). He wanted no biography written and his second wife, Sonia Brownell, who was the legal guardian to his literary estate, carried out these wishes for three decades. The official biography in 1980 did not mention prostitutes or drugs (Crick 1992 [1980]). When Major Wellborne, a high-ranking Deputy Inspector-General in the police establishment, called Eric Blair 'a disgrace to Eton College' in front of his peers at the club in Katha, did he know more than Orwell's biographers about his behaviour in Burma (Stuart: Orwell Archive)?

We will never know with certainty how Eric Blair, as a young Assistant Superintendent Police Officer, spent his off-duty hours in Burma. From slender evidence, biographers have concluded that he enjoyed the company of married women and prostitutes, perhaps becoming sterile due to venereal disease (Bowker 2003: 82; Shelden 1997: 108-109; Sutherland 2016: 98-100). There is indiscrete conversation reported in a memoir (Acton 1986 [1970]: 153), *Burmese Days* and a few lines in his poetry and not much other evidence. Considering he is a young man with few available women, it is not difficult to imagine Orwell would have sex where possible. It should be noted that Beadon was fooled, '…as for female company, I don't honestly think I ever saw him with a woman' (Coppard 1984: 65). There is nearly as much circumstantial evidence indicating experimentation with opium during these off-duty hours.

Orwell knew he needed to hide his behaviour from others. Fellow Etonian, the conservative Catholic Christopher Hollis, on visiting Orwell in Rangoon during 1925, found a completely orthodox young police officer (Hollis 2017 [1956]: 27-28). One biographer believes this was the impression Orwell purposefully wanted to give Hollis who was returning to England and would undoubtedly discuss his trip with people who knew the Old Etonian (Bowker 2003: 86). It is telling that Beadon acknowledges that '…to find that George Orwell was Eric A. Blair, as I say, was rather like seeing a flying saucer arrive at your front door…' (Coppard 1984: 65).

Opium then? A 'lower-upper-middle-class' man who was prepared to go down a coal mine with working men, get himself purposefully arrested, associate with a criminal underclass in Paris and London, spend time with the poor and homeless as well as risking his life in a time of civil war in Spain would surely not have baulked at smoking opium, if the opportunity presented itself, especially considering the nature of his father's work.

Orwell's writing reveals familiarity with the effects of drugs. Find your copy of 'A Hanging' (1931) and read it again. It's more a dreamy, stunningly visual short story, than an essay, exploring an experience of sudden death. The narrator seems barely present while watching the 'sodden morning of rains' and 'sickly light like yellow tinfoil' fall on the 'condemned cells' (*CWGO* X 1998: 417). There are drug references or moments in most of his nine standard published works. These are often minor but some not yet mentioned in this paper are worth highlighting.

Orwell's allegoric fable, *Animal Farm* (1945) concludes with a memorable scene. The corpulent pig, Napoleon, announces that the name 'Animal Farm' had been abolished and 'Manor Farm' – the correct and original name – is to be reinstated. The pigs drain their glasses in a toast. The long-suffering animals look through the window at the strange scene of pigs, standing on two legs, consorting with men, their enemies:

> But as the animals outside gazed at the scene, it seemed to them that some strange thing was happening. What was it that had altered in the faces of the pigs? Clover's old dim eyes flitted from one face to another. Some of them had five chins, some had four, some had three. But what was it that seemed to be melting and changing? ... No question, now, what had happened to the faces of the pigs. The creatures outside looked from pig to man, and from man to pig, and from pig to man again; but already it was impossible to say which was which. (Orwell 1945: 91-92)

If Thomas de Quincey had written this, his knowledge of opium-eating would be used to explain the visually vivid image of faces 'melting and changing'. Orwell owned a copy of Thomas De Quincey's, *Confessions of an English Opium Eater* (1821) and reviewed books about Baudelaire (*The Adelphi* 1933), another opium-eater, as well as collecting pamphlets about opium (British Library 1939: 1899.ss.12). Transformation, in literature, especially fairy tales, is nothing new but this is a stunningly poignant example.

Nineteen Eighty-Four (1949) has the protagonist agreeing 'to distribute habit-forming drugs, to encourage prostitution, to disseminate venereal diseases...' (Orwell 1949: 173) before being given Goldstein's manifesto which mentions 'the truth-producing effects of drugs' (ibid: 195). Near the end of the novel, Winston Smith falls into a strange, blissful reverie where 'everything was settled, smoothed out, reconciled. There were no more doubts, no more arguments, no more pain, no more fear ... in the delirium induced by drugs. He was in the Golden Country' (ibid: 280). A caption – for what is likely the last photograph of Orwell – may be hyperbolic in suggesting that he 'foretold … mind-changing drugs' (Man 1984 [1983]) but he does write with apparent experience rather than theoretical knowledge.

Did Orwell smoke opium in Burma? There is no conclusive proof. His reportage and fiction suggest he experimented with drugs, as have others of every literary generation (Boon 2002: 7). Orwell was not willing to dishonour the name of Richard Blair by writing about the opium trade, or possibly, his own experimentation. The fact that he named his adopted son 'Richard' displayed a loving commitment to his father's memory. George Orwell was addicted to tobacco and tea, nothing stronger but it is possible, while exploring the rich tapestry of life, indulged in other 'indescribable' pleasures.

NOTE

[1] A separate paper detailing information gleaned from these diaries is currently in preparation

REFERENCES

Abbott, Gerry (2006) Robbie and the Poet, *SOAS*, Vol. 4, No. 1 pp 45-47. Available online at http://www.burmalibrary.org/docs11/SBBR4.1-Abbott.pdf, accessed on 14 September 2018

Acton, Harold (1986 [1970]) *More Memoirs of an Aesthete,* London: Hamish Hamilton

Ancestry.com (n. d.) UK, Registers of Employees of the East India Company and the India Office, 1746-1939/University of London; India List Civil and Military India; Reference Number: b2168330~S10 1890 pt 1

Baker, Phil (2018) Unpublished paper

Binns, Ronald (2018) *Orwell in Southwold*, Great Britain: Zoilus Press

Blair, Eric Arthur (1931) A Hanging, *CWGO* 10 pp 207-10. Originally published *The Adelphi,* Vol. 2, No. 5, August

Blair, Eric Arthur (1933) Review: Enid Starkie's *Baudelaire*, *CWGO* 10 pp 320-21. Originally published *The Adelphi,* Vol. 6, No. 5, August

Boon, Marcus (2002) *The Road of Excess – A History of Writers on Drugs*, London: Harvard University Press

Bowker, Gordon (2003) *George Orwell*, London: Little, Brown

Bowker, Gordon (2007) George Orwell: A paranoid rebel with tattoos on his knuckles, *Guardian*, 5 September. Available online at https://www.theguardian.com/books/2007/sep/05/georgeorwell, accessed on 5 September 2018

British Library (1922) E. A. Blair's recruitment file: India Office Records L/PJ/6/1827 6079/1922

British Library (1939) Opium: Japan's Big Weapon of War, *A collection of pamphlets, mainly political, formed by George Orwell*, 1899.ss.12

Buddicom, Jacintha (2006 [1974]) *Eric and Us*, Finlay Publishers, postscript edition

Chopra, Ram Nath and Chopra, I. C. (1955) UNODC: Bulletin on Narcotics, *Unodc.org*. Available online at: https://www.unodc.org/unodc/en/data-and-analysis/bulletin/bulletin_1955-01-01_3_page002.html, accessed on 1 October 2018

Colls, Robert (2013) *George Orwell: English Rebel*, Oxford: Oxford University Press

Coppard, Audrey and Crick, Bernard (1984) *Orwell Remembered,* London: Ariel Books/BBC

Crick, Bernard (1992 [1980]) *George Orwell: A Life,* Harmondsworth, Middlesex: Penguin, second edition

Davison, Peter (2010) *George Orwell: Diaries*, New York: Liveright

Deming, Sarah (2011) The economic importance of Indian opium and trade with China on Britain's economy, 1843-1890, *Whitman College, Economics Working Papers*, No. 25, Spring. Available online at https://www.whitman.edu/Documents/Academics/Economics/Working%20Paper%20Contents/WP_25.pdf, accessed on 20 September 2018

Discovery.nationalarchives.gov.uk. (2018) Special Branch file on Eric Blair alias George Orwell, author and journalist, *The National Archives*, MEPO 38/69. Available online at http://discovery.nationalarchives.gov.uk/details/r/C10881756, accessed on 22 September 2018

Hollis, Christopher (2017 [1956]) *A Study of George Orwell: The Man and His Works*, New York: Racehorse Publishing

Harrap and Co. (1941) Book Contract

Honchell, Stephanie (2010) *Pursuing pleasure, attaining oblivion: The roles and uses of intoxicants at the Mughal court*. Electronic Theses and Dissertations. Paper 628. Available online at: https://doi.org/10.18297/etd/628

Inglis, Lucy (2018) *Milk of Paradise: A History of Opium*, London: Pan Macmillan

Kingdom-Ward, Frank (1924) *From China to Hkamti Long*, London: Edward Arnold & Co.

Larkin, Emma (2011) *Finding George Orwell in Burma*, Cambridge: Granta

London Gazette (1924) 30 May

Man, Felix, H. (1984 [1983]) *Man With Camera: Photographs from Seven Decades*, London: Schoken Books

Meer-Nemo, A. (1969) *A Burma Bobby*, Unpublished Manuscript, British Library: Mss Eur C499

Meyers, Jeffrey (2000*) Orwell: Wintry Conscience of a Generation*, New York: W. W. Norton & Co.

Moore, Darcy (2018) *The Diaries of Henry Osborne*. Available online at http://www.darcymoore.net/tag/henry-osborne/ Blog Posts

Orwell, George (1945) *Animal Farm*, London: Martin Secker & Warburg Ltd.

Orwell, George (1949) *Nineteen Eighty-four*, London: Martin Secker & Warburg Ltd.

Orwell, George (1997 [1933]) *Down and Out in London and Paris, The Complete Works of George Orwell, Vol.1,* London: Secker & Warburg pp 124-126

Orwell, George (1997 [1934]) *Burmese Days, The Complete Works of George Orwell, Vol. 2,* London: Secker & Warburg pp 132-133, 309

Orwell, George (1997 [1935]) *A Clergyman's Daughter, The Complete Works of George Orwell, Vol. 3,* London: Secker & Warburg p. 46

Orwell, George (1997 [1937]) *The Road to Wigan Pier, The Complete Works of George Orwell, Vol. 5,* London: Secker & Warburg p. 72

DARCY MOORE

Orwell, George (1998 [1942]) Review: *A Modern De Quincey*, *The Complete Works of George Orwell, Vol. 14*, Davison, Peter (ed.) London: Secker & Warburg pp 34-35. originally published *Observer*, 13 September

Osborne, Henry (1876-1905) *Diaries of Henry Osborne, Sub-Deputy Opium Agent for the Opium Department, India Office, of the British Government in Bengal Province, India*, London: Lett's Diaries Company, Ltd

Richards, Vernon (1998) *George Orwell at Home (and Among the Anarchists): Essays and Photographs*, London: Freedom Press

Rahman, Maseeh (2014) George Orwell's birthplace in India set to become a museum, *Guardian*, 4 June. Available online at https://www.theguardian.com/world/2014/jun/30/george-orwell-birthplace-motihari-bihar-india-museum, accessed on 5 September 2018

Rivett-Carnac, John Henry (1910) *Many Memories of Life in India, at Home, and Abroad*, Edinburgh and London: William Blackwood and Sons

Robinson, Capt. H. R. (1942) *A Modern De Quincey – An Autobiography*, London: George G. Harrap and Co.

Robinson, Captain H. R. (2004 [1942]) *A Modern De Quincey: An Autobiography of an Opium Addict*, Bangkok: Orchid Press, second edition

Rowntree, Joshua (1895) *The Opium Habit in the East: A Study Of The Evidence Given To The Royal Commission On Opium 1893-4*, Westminster: P. S. King & Son

Shelden, Michael (1991) *Orwell: The Authorised Biography*, London: Heinemann

Stansky, Peter and Abrahams, William (1972) *The Unknown Orwell,* New York: Alfred A. Knopf

Stansky, Peter and Abrahams, William (1980) *Orwell: The Transformation*, New York: Alfred A. Knopf

Stuart, George (n. d.) Interview (audio-cassette), Orwell Archive

Sutherland, John (2016) *Orwell's Nose*, London: Reaktion Books

Starkie, Enid (1971) *Baudelaire*, Great Britain: Pelican Biographies

Taylor, D. J. (2004 [2003]) *Orwell – The Life*, London: Vintage

Taylor, D. J. (2018) Don't fear that I will leave your letter lying about: George Orwell's notes for his lover, *Times*, 10 July. Available online at https://www.thetimes.co.uk/article/dont-fear-that-i-will-leave-your-letter-lying-about-george-orwells-notes-for-his-lover-pql7mf8cj, accessed on 5 September 2018

The Burma Opium Manual, 1925 (1927) Rangoon: Government Printing

Wadhams, Stephen (1983) Unpublished Recordings from CBC Radio (courtesy of the Orwell Society)

Wadhams, Stephen (1984) *Remembering Orwell,* Harmondsworth, Middlesex: Penguin

Williams, Raymond (1974) *Orwell*, London: Fontana

NOTE ON THE CONTRIBUTOR

Darcy Moore is a deputy principal at a secondary school in New South Wales. He teaches English and History and has worked as an academic in post-graduate teacher education at the University of Wollongong. His interest in Orwell began at school, thirty-five years ago, when he was enthralled by *Animal Farm* and *Nineteen Eighty-Four*. He is currently working on a book about Orwell and drugs. He blogs at darcymoore.net and his Twitter handle is @Darcy1968. His Orwell collection can be accessed at darcymoore.net/orwell-collection/

PAPER

Orwell as Social Patriot – and British Cinema Studies

MARTIN STOLLERY

This paper considers how Orwell has been employed by some writers within the field of British cinema studies, particularly those whose work reaches out to a wider readership beyond academic disciplinary boundaries. It explores how a relatively narrow figuration of Orwell as an English social patriot has been deployed within this context. It demonstrates how this is based upon a selective appropriation of quotations from The Lion and the Unicorn, *reinforced by this key text's publishing history, which do not do justice to the range and incisiveness of Orwell's analysis of British imperial culture. It argues that British cinema studies would benefit from also acknowledging the divergence between the positions Orwell developed on empire, particularly in his wartime radio work, and mainstream trends within 1930s and 1940s British media.*

Keywords: Orwell, British cinema, Ealing studios, Humphrey Jennings, film studies

Most Orwell scholars agree that in the sixty-eight years since his death his name has been put to varying uses in a wide range of fields, for example in political discourse and cultural analysis, where *Nineteen Eighty-Four* (1949) and selected essays are key reference points respectively. My aim in this paper is to consider some of the ways Orwell has figured within British cinema studies and to propose a new approach. I focus on two examples. The first is Charles Barr's book *Ealing Studios* (first published in 1977), one of the founding texts of British cinema studies, about the 1940s and 1950s output of the studio commemorated, on its 1955 sale to the BBC, by a plaque celebrating its production of 'many films projecting Britain and the British character'. The second example is critical discussion of documentary film maker Humphrey Jennings, famously described by Lindsay Anderson as 'the only real poet the British cinema has yet produced' (Anderson 2004a: 359).

Barr not only quotes and references Orwell several times during *Ealing Studios*, he also declares: 'I am not writing this book with George Orwell's works at my elbow for inspiration, but it is hard to immerse oneself in Ealing without being repeatedly reminded

MARTIN STOLLERY

of this writer' (1993 [1977]: 90). Barr posits the affinity between Orwell and Ealing as one that occurred to him during the process of writing his book, rather than suggesting that Orwell's work had a direct impact upon Ealing's film makers during the 1940s and 1950s. During this earlier period, Orwell's name did not enjoy the visibility, prestige and authority it had attained by the time Barr wrote *Ealing Studios*, in the wake of the publication, in 1968, of the four-volume *The Collected Essays, Journalism and Letters of George Orwell* (edited by Sonia Orwell and Ian Angus). As Peter Marks puts it, this collection 'propelled Orwell to the forefront of public intellectuals whose ideas were worth quoting and discussing, significantly broadening his public and scholarly appeal' (2011: 195). At the same time, *Animal Farm* (1945) and *Nineteen Eighty-Four* continued to sell in quantities that would have been unimaginable when Orwell died in 1950; more than twenty million paperback copies by the beginning of the 1970s (Rodden 2017 [2001]: 49).

Nearly a decade after *Ealing Studios* first appeared, Barr (1986) published an influential essay that traced and challenged the history of critical neglect and downright dismissal of British cinema. Within this context of perceived neglect and dismissal, Barr's use of Orwell in *Ealing Studios* can be compared to Robin Wood's provocative analogy between William Shakespeare's dramas and the Hollywood films directed by Alfred Hitchcock in his ground-breaking *Hitchcock's Films* (first published in 1965). Wood's Shakespeare reference occurs in his introductory chapter which begins with the question: 'Why should we take Hitchcock seriously?' (Wood 2002: 55). Barr's style is different to Wood's; nevertheless, one of *Ealing Studios'* implicit assertions is that if we take Orwell seriously we should take the films Barr discusses seriously as well. Significantly, Wood, who studied English Literature at Cambridge, and Barr, who contributed to the Cambridge literary magazine *Granta*, were the two critics loosely associated with *Movie* magazine in the 1960s most familiar with literary criticism (Gibbs 2013: 150-151). Both went on to establish film studies programmes within university literature departments (at the University of Warwick and University of East Anglia respectively) in the mid-1970s. Barr's references to Orwell are, therefore, explicable on a number of levels.

The master metaphor Barr derives from Orwell is in a passage he quotes from *The Lion and the Unicorn* (1941):

> England ... is a family in which the young are generally thwarted and most of the power is in the hands of irresponsible uncles and bedridden aunts. Still, it is a family. It has its private language and its common memories, and at the approach of an enemy it closes its ranks (Orwell 1998a [1941]: 401; Barr 1993 [1977]: 14).

Barr traces the emergent theme of 'England as a family', pulling together and closing ranks, in early Ealing films produced by Michael Balcon such as *Cheer Boys Cheer* (Walter Forde, 1939), and the wartime *San Demetrio, London* (Charles Frend, 1943). *The Ladykillers* (Alexander Mackendrick, 1955), in which 'bedridden aunts' reassert their power during the more stagnant 1950s, is for him the most darkly comic realisation of the the other part of Orwell's formula, which is that 'wrong members' of the English family are in control (Orwell 1998a: 401). Barr also argues that the affective resonance of the quotidian English 'landscapes' invoked in *The Lion and the Unicorn* – 'we are a nation … of stamp collectors, pigeon-fanciers, amateur carpenters, coupon-snippers, darts players, crossword puzzle fans … the pub, the football match, the back garden, the fireside and the "nice cup of tea"' (ibid: 394; Barr 1993 [1977]: 90) – is paralleled in Ealing films such as *The Blue Lamp* (Basil Dearden, 1950). In one of *Ealing Studios*' most inspired passages, Barr extrapolates from Orwell's remarks about the unaesthetic English 'love of flowers' to discuss how *The Blue Lamp* delicately employs a flower (and manure) motif to eulogise affable policeman George Dixon's (Jack Warner's) 'unambitious daily routine that has its own modest satisfactions' after he is shockingly murdered (ibid: 94).

Film maker and critic Lindsay Anderson offered a very different assessment of this sequence in *The Blue Lamp* where Mrs Dixon (Gladys Henson), on hearing of her husband's murder, simply says: 'I'll just put these flowers in water.' Anderson considered it 'so bottled up that [emotions] have ceased to exist at all' (2004b: 235). However, although Anderson's assessment of individual films differed from Barr's, Orwell was also an important reference point for Anderson throughout his career, as was Humphrey Jennings. Anderson did not link them directly in his published writings, but valued both for similar reasons. Anderson was one of the British intellectuals who boosted Orwell's reputation during the 1950s. In the same 1957 essay in which he decried *The Blue Lamp*, Anderson mourned the lost wartime spirit of 'comradeship and mutual aid' and argued that Orwell's comments in *The Lion and the Unicorn* about most leftist intellectuals' 'snobbishness' and 'severance from the common culture of the country' still held true in the 1950s (2004b [1957]: 248). Three years earlier, Anderson identified Jennings and the wartime films he directed at the Crown Film Unit as embodying the values he admired in Orwell. He praised the films for epitomising how, 'in a country at war we are all members of one another', and celebrated Jennings for his 'freedom from the inhibitions of class-consciousness' and 'fascination with the commonplace thing or person precisely because it is commonplace' (2004a [1954]: 361; 364; 360).

MARTIN STOLLERY

The Humphrey Jennings Film Reader, published in 1993, edited by Kevin Jackson, included an extract from a letter Jennings wrote to his wife Cicely, in May 1941, in which Jennings praised Orwell's 'excellent analysis' in *The Lion and the Unicorn* of British intellectuals who were afraid of becoming 'patriots' (Jennings 1993 [1941]: 29). This encouraged further direct comparisons between Orwell and Jennings, especially in Jackson's 2004 biography of the latter. Jackson speculates about the 'tantalising possibility' of a possible 'youthful encounter' between Jennings (1907-1950) and Orwell (1903-1950) when they were living in Walberswick and Southwold respectively, close to each other in Suffolk (2004: 10). He describes *Spare Time* (1939), generally considered an important early work in Jennings' development as a film maker, as demonstrating 'affinities with that other eloquent connoisseur of boys' comics, dirty postcards, pub life and other manifestations of democratic industrial folkways, George Orwell' (2004: 214).

Similarly, Jackson argues that the last film Jennings completed, *Family Portrait* (1950), employs Orwell's *The Lion and the Unicorn* metaphor of Britain as a 'deeply divided family' (2004: 349). Jackson's biography, like Barr's *Ealing Studios*, and Anderson's critical writing, was pitched at and has resonated with a wider audience than solely an academic one. The usefulness of Orwell as a reference point in Jackson's campaign to raise Jennings' wider public profile is evident in the titles of some of the magazine and newspaper articles he published while working on his biography, such as 'The Orwell of cinema' (Jackson 1999; 2001). Some subsequent publications on Jennings' work followed suit by exploring affinities and parallels with Orwell (Beattie 2010; Hunter 2010).

ORWELL AND FILM STUDIES

It would be difficult to dispute the contributions Barr, Anderson and Jackson have made to the study of British cinema, but none of them fit entirely comfortably into standard accounts of the emergence of film studies as an academic discipline. Two of them, Anderson and Jackson, wrote as freelance journalists rather than academics, and the former was trenchantly opposed to what he saw as the emergent discipline of film studies' pointlessly abstruse idioms and preoccupations. For all three, their positive references to Orwell combine with general adherence to the precepts outlined in his essay 'Politics and the English language' (1946) regarding the use of 'language as an instrument for expressing and not for concealing or preventing thought' (1998c [1946]: 430). According to taste, their work can be praised for contributing to but also being accessible to readers outside the specialised discipline of film studies, or it can be critiqued for lacking theoretical rigour.

Some historians of film studies, within and beyond the university, such as Lee Grieveson and Haidee Wasson, have rightly warned against citing 'the May 1968 period and the intellectual and political contexts from which it grew' as marking 'the birth of the discipline' (2008: xv). Barr's trajectory, as one of the founders of British university film studies, is sufficient to give the lie to this assumption within the British context. Nevertheless, as film studies as an academic discipline expanded across the British university sector during the 1970s and 1980s, what later became known as *Screen* theory (insofar as the journal of that name was its most visible proponent) occupied a leading role. As Grieveson and Wasson note, 'disciplinisation itself … necessarily creates hierarchies of valued work' (2008: xvi). The work widely considered most cutting-edge and valuable within film studies during this period adopted a language and set of references different from Anderson's and Barr's more traditionally humanist registers, for reasons outlined by Phillip Rosen:

> In rereading *Screen* and its allies now, one is struck by the extent to which the search for new thinking was in the air at the time. Desires for radical political novelty at the end of the 1960s corresponded with a quest for radical transformation among some intellectual sectors. Notions of fundamental change, epistemological breaks, and, occasionally, revolution were the order of the day. This coalesced with the growing and controversial prestige of theory as a mode by which to renovate Anglo-American critical studies within the academy. All of these fed into ambitions to overhaul film theory along with film culture (2008: 265).

A more negative perspective on this development is that theoretical discussion could ossify into what Richard Dyer has called a 'terrifying language of authority', characterised by what Orwell criticised as 'pretentious diction' (Grant and Kooijman 2016; Orwell 1998c [1946]: 424). Within this context, Orwell could become either an exemplar of theoretical naivety or a touchstone for lucidity.

Raymond Williams provides a graphic example of the former perception of Orwell within the post-May 1968 period. In his late 1970s dialogue with *New Left Review* editors Perry Anderson, Anthony Barnett, and Francis Mulhern, Williams tacitly accepted their assertion that Orwell did not 'produce new theoretical knowledge about society or history', and concluded that he 'cannot bear much of [Orwell's work] now. If I had to say which writings have done the most damage, it would be what you call the social patriotism – the dreadful stuff from the beginning of the war about England as a family with the wrong members in charge' (1979: 391-392). Within the parallel realm of theoretically-orientated academic work on British cinema, Orwell was often either not mentioned or relegated below newly established reference points. One example is *National Fictions: World War Two in British Films and Television* (1984), an influential collection of essays which encompassed discussion of some Ealing films, such as *The Bells Go Down* (1943). As the collection's editor Geoff Hurd emphasised in his contribution, the 'view of wartime cinema' developed in *National Fictions* was 'derived directly from Antonio Gramsci's concept of hegemony' (1984: 18). A later example of this type of approach is Tony Williams's book *Structures of Desire: British Cinema, 1939-1955* (2000). Covering broadly the same period as Barr's *Ealing Studios*, and focusing on a number of Ealing films, Williams cites Gramsci's concept of hegemony, and Raymond Williams's further development of this concept, as his main theoretical coordinates. *Structures of Desire* does include references to Orwell, but these are not as central to its argument as the aforementioned theorists.

As far as Jennings was concerned, Andrew Britton's dissenting 1989 essay argued that British wartime unity, taken for granted in Anderson's celebration of this film maker, involved cultural negotiation between conflicting values and a temporary compromise equilibrium between competing classes structurally opposed to each other:

> British war unity was characterised not by the suspension of class struggle or class politics but, on the contrary, by the British ruling class's recognition that it could not pursue its own war aim – to wit, the crushing of Germany's resistance to the hegemony of British imperialism – without making major political concessions to its own domestic class antagonist, large sections of which were intensely hostile to prewar Toryism in general and Churchill, in particular (2009: 304).

For Britton, films directed by Jennings, such as *Fires Were Started* (1943) and *A Diary for Timothy* (1945), promoted a reductive and reactionary notion of national unity rather than addressing class antagonisms. Other academic critics during this period demurred, arguing that the wartime films directed by Jennings, particularly *Listen to Britain* (co-directed with Stewart McAllister 1942), were not as univocal as Britton suggested (Nowell-Smith 1986). The key point is that these discussions of British wartime cinema, often conducted within the ambit of Gramsci's concept of hegemony, implicitly challenged Orwell's assertion in *The Lion and the Unicorn* that England was a fractious but fundamentally unified family. For theorists such as Hurd and Britton, conceiving the nation as a family was itself part of the hegemonic process. As Raymond Williams put it: 'The difficulty, surely, lies in the original image of the family. Orwell hated what he saw of the consequences of capitalism, but he was never able to see it, fully, as an economic and political *system*' (1984: 26).

PRIESTLEY AND FILM HISTORY

Barr's references to Orwell's sometimes neglected peer J. B. Priestley can also be situated in relation to other developments within the academic discipline of film studies. Barr identifies Priestley in *Ealing Studios* as having a clear affinity and direct relationship with the studio before and after Balcon's tenure. However, Orwell occupies a more central role within the book's structure. One of the chapters begins with an Orwell quotation as an epigraph, and Barr uses particular images from *The Lion and the Unicorn* as leitmotifs throughout *Ealing Studios*. Priestley's critical standing, although recently elevated by the publication of new editions of some of his work, and the appearance of several new academic studies, has always been lower than Orwell's since the latter became enshrined within the English literary canon from the 1950s onwards. Hence, when *Ealing Studios* was published in the 1970s, it made sense to align the studio's output more closely with Orwell than with Priestley for the purpose of establishing its cultural significance.

Alongside *Screen* theory, another way in which film studies was validated as a discipline was through the serious pursuit of historical research. The foundation of the *Historical Journal of Film, Radio and Television* in 1981 is often taken as one of the early markers of this trend, which has in many instances has been integrated with rather than opposed to aspects of *Screen* theory. By the turn of the millennium, film studies was firmly established as an academic discipline, accommodating different methodologies and distinctive individual voices. British cinema had become a recognised topic within the discipline, and *Ealing Studios* was ensconced on reading lists as a key text. Barr's 2005 essay on Ealing's and the Crown Film Unit's prehistory, therefore, did not need to validate its subject matter and reversed the priority accorded to Orwell and Priestley in *Ealing Studios*. Barr notes Orwell's dismissive or patronising attitude towards Priestley, and then goes on to argue that the first film version of *The Good Companions* (1933), adapted from Priestley's best-selling novel and its stage adaptation, prefigured the theme of striving for 'more genuine versions of community and companionship' that came to fruition in wartime Ealing and Crown Film Unit films (2005: 34).

Barr also traces a continuity between Priestley's celebration of 'true community' and the production method of *The Good Companions*, with its innovative screen credit listing Angus MacPhail, Ian Dalrymple, George Gunn and Louis Levy, specialists in scriptwriting, editing, music and sound respectively, described on-screen at the start of the film as 'production personnel', an undifferentiated team of film makers (2005: 38). Barr sees this as an anticipation of Balcon's, *The Good Companions*' producer's, later attempt to run Ealing as 'the studio with the team spirit', and as foreshadowing the relatively egalitarian production dynamics Dalrymple sought to foster at the Crown Film Unit.

MARTIN STOLLERY

In *Ealing Studios*, Barr argues that it took Balcon 'until about 1942 to pick and train a team which could respond to Britain's war experience with the kind of inspirational feature most appropriate to it – films like *The Foreman Went to France*, *Nine Men*, and *San Demetrio, London* – which embody classic British qualities of team spirit and good-humoured doggedness' (op cit: 13). Priestley was credited for the story on which *The Foreman Went to France* was based. Two years later Ealing adapted his successful stage play *They Came to a City*. The narrative involves the reactions of nine socially diverse characters mysteriously transported to the gate of a city that is potentially a socialist utopia. The film foregrounds Priestley's authorship; he appears in a framing story, where he relates the narrative to a young couple debating postwar Britain's future. As Jo Botting puts it, the fantastic set in the main narrative emphasises the nine characters' 'role as pawns in a game of Priestley's devising, the floor in front of the gate decorated like a huge chess board' (2012: 180).

Priestley was much more visible and influential than Orwell during the Second World War, familiar to a wide audience after his first series of 1940 BBC radio *Postscript* broadcasts. *They Came to a City* attempts to capitalise on this. One overly optimistic mid-1940s commentator saw so much consonance that he predicted Ealing 'will probably in future make one Priestley picture a year' (Noble 1946: 88). However, *They Came to a City* was not well served by distributors, and was not a box office success. Nevertheless, any historical account of the sources of adapted material and the direct impact of literary figures on Ealing during the 1940s would need to give a significant role to Priestley but would hardly feature Orwell at all.

THE LION AND THE UNICORN, BRITISH CINEMA AND THE EMPIRE

The uses to which Orwell has been put within British cinema studies, especially in texts such as *Ealing Studios* and Jackson's biography of Jennings, aimed at general as well as academic readers, have in some respects been selective and derivative of established emphases. Raymond Williams has gone so far as to argue of the 'family with the wrong members in control' metaphor that 'Orwell's great influence since the 1940s owes as much to this powerful image as to any other single achievement' (1984: 22). Williams explains its longevity by suggesting that it meshed with British Labour Party revisionism of the 1950s and 1960s which promoted 'pragmatic social reform' and the advancement of a new meritocracy (1984: 84), or, in Orwell's terms, the handing of control to more progressive family members, rather than confronting and dismantling deep-rooted structural inequalities. Williams also suggests that Orwell remained influential, at least during the early phases of the New Left and the emergence of cultural studies, because he 'tried to live and feel where the majority of English people were living and feeling: reporting, understanding, respecting beyond the range of Establishment culture' (1984: 85). This encompasses the quotidian cultural landscapes, invoked in *The Lion and the Unicorn* and other essays, which Barr, Anderson and Jackson describe as Orwellian in films such as *The Blue Lamp* and *Spare Time*.

Overwhelmingly, the Orwell quotations used by certain writers within British cinema studies not only derive from *The Lion and the Unicorn*, but more specifically from 'England Your England', the first of the pamphlet's three main sections. This narrowing of focus has been reinforced by the text's publication history. An essay later incorporated into 'England Your England' initially appeared in *Horizon* magazine in December 1940. This essay, 'The Ruling Class', offered a balanced yet incisive critique of this 'unteachable', dominant sector of British society at the outbreak of war, whose 'money and power' needed to be 'gone', although Orwell does not specify how this will be achieved (Orwell 1940: 323). At this early stage the family metaphor is absent. It does not appears until the 'England Your England' section of *The Lion and the Unicorn*, first published in February 1941, when Orwell moved beyond critique of the ruling class to try to articulate a positive basis for winning the war and transforming British society. Soon after Orwell's death, 'England Your England' became the privileged section of *The Lion and the Unicorn*. It was reprinted as a stand alone essay, detached from the subsequent two sections, in the Orwell collections *England Your England* and *Such Were the Joys*, published in 1953 in Britain and America respectively. *The Orwell Reader*, first published in 1956, likewise reprinted 'England Your England' rather than the other two thirds of *The Lion and the Unicorn*.

Peter Marks (2011) has emphasised the importance of considering how different readers within different contexts have approached Orwell through various editions of his work and collections of his essays, which do not necessarily follow the chronological arc of his career, and which sometimes omit or minimise discussion of when or where they first appeared. Marks reminds us of the 'periodical culture' of the 1930s and 1940s to which Orwell was a contributor, and of the circumstances in which his essays were initially published. These considerations do not provide the key to the true meaning of these texts; posthumous publications and collections of Orwell's work reached far wider readerships than in his lifetime, and need to be given equal if not more weight in any balanced analysis of his work's cultural and historical impact. Nevertheless, attending to the circumstances of *The Lion and the Unicorn*'s initial publication can open up new perspectives on Orwell and British cinema. Rather than narrowing this text to a few repetitively cited quotations from its 'England Your England' section, I will consider the environment in which it initially circulated, when it was first issued as part of the *Searchlight Books* series.

MARTIN STOLLERY

As John Newsinger (1999) has pointed out, *The Lion and the Unicorn* was part of a broader cultural intervention during the early war years that extended beyond a single text. It was the first in a series of 128-page extended essays, published by Secker and Warburg, which Orwell co-edited with Tosco Fyvel, each with a distinctive searchlight motif on the front cover, designed by Phillip Zec. *Searchlight Books,* partly modelled on the sixpence *Penguin Specials*, retailed at two shillings a copy. Advertising for the series featured an endorsement from J. B. Priestley, confirming his status as one of the most visible public intellectuals on the left. The statement of intent for the series extended far beyond the selected quotations from 'England Your England' that are now overly familiar through repetition. The series was designed to:

> Criticise and kill what is rotten in Western civilization and supply constructive ideas for the difficult time ahead of us. The series … will stress Britain's international and imperial responsibilities and the aim of a planned Britain at the head of a great and freer British Commonwealth and linked with the United States of America as a framework of world order (cited in Costello 1989: 257).

As part of its 'international and imperial' purview, the series included Sebastian Haffner's *Offensive against Germany* (1941), which considered German morale and public opinion, Arturo Barea's *Struggle for the Spanish Soul* (1941) and Joyce Cary's *The Struggle for African Freedom* (1941). Considering *The Lion and the Unicorn* within this context prompts a shift of attention away from its first, 'England, Your England' section towards its third, 'The English Revolution'. In this overlooked section, Orwell outlined a six-point programme, three of which 'deal with England's internal policy, the other three with the Empire and the world' (1998a [1941]: 422). The fourth point is: 'Immediate Dominion status for India, with power to secede when the war is over' (ibid), and he goes on to argue that 'what applies to India applies, *mutatis mutandis*, to Burma, Malaya and most of our African possessions' (ibid: 426). There is some powerful writing in this section, but imagery such as the 'stream of dividends that flows from the bodies of Indian coolies to the banking accounts of old ladies in Cheltenham' (ibid: 425) has not acquired the same cultural resonance as Orwell's 'family' metaphor, partly because it cannot so easily be assimilated to consensual or comedic understandings of England. Orwell's friend and colleague Mulk Raj Anand wrote in 1941 of a British 'blind spot' in relation to India (cited in West 1987: 15); this description can be applied to the uses to which *The Lion and the Unicorn*, or rather its first section, has been put.

Paul Gilroy persuasively argues that Orwell has been 'wrongly and routinely recuperated in traditions of political culture that are far too nation-centred and narrowly patriotic. His experiences in Burma, Spain, and Paris have not been made useful in the same ways as his peregrinations inside Britain' (2004: 87-88). Gilroy tends to focus on examples of Orwell's writing from before the Second World War, especially his review essay, 'Not Counting Niggers', first published in July 1939, in which he denounced imperialism as a 'far vaster injustice' than fascism and highlighted the hypocrisy of anti-fascists who overlooked it (1998b [1939]: 360). Newsinger, on the other hand, points out that none of the wartime *Searchlight Books* were as trenchant as this, and concludes that Orwell probably 'did not regard such public indictments of the British Empire as helpful when Britain was fighting for her survival' (Newsinger 1999: 85). There is certainly a less strident tone after the outbreak of war, and by 1944 Orwell accepted that fascism was the greater evil (Newsinger 2018: 65). Nevertheless, *The Lion and the Unicorn*, in its evocation of how India is imbricated in supposedly quintessentially English lifestyles, such as comfortable retirement in a regency spa town, demonstrates what Gilroy describes as 'a worldly consciousness ... articulated in strict harmony with Orwell's parochial attachments to England's distinctive environment' (2004: 85).

This opens up a different perspective on Orwell and British cinema, which can be further illuminated by considering Wendy Webster's work on representations of empire and Englishness. Webster's analysis of cinema, television, radio and other media during and after the Second World War identifies several strands of rhetoric and imagery, which can intersect in particular texts. Webster contrasts Winston Churchill's public image, for example, as personifying 'martial masculinity associated with empire', calling 'the nation to heroic deeds associated with imperial identity', with Priestley's image, which invokes the 'temperate hero', linked to the 'common people characterised by humour and quiet courage, by modest domestic pleasures and homely comforts, and particularly by kindness' (2005: 38, 36). In short, Churchill's cigar contrasts with Priestley's pipe. Another strand Webster identifies is 'people's empire' rhetoric and imagery, extending the notion of the 'people's war' by representing 'a heterogeneous people pulling together across differences of race and ethnicity, united in a common cause' (ibid: 22). Nationalist aspirations within the British empire, Japanese propaganda challenging British imperialism and American reservations about British imperial rule encouraged an emphasis upon 'themes of partnership and welfare' in 'people's empire' representations (ibid: 29).

These three strands broadly correlate to particular types and cycles of British film-making during the late 1930s and wartime period. The first is the imperial adventure film, including examples such as *Sanders of the River* (1935) and *The Four Feathers* (1939). However, as Prem Chowdhry has argued, the protests occasioned by the release in India of *The Drum* (1938), a modern day imperial adventure narrative about a rebellion against British rule, followed by the outbreak of war, brought home to British and American film producers the need to tread warily in relation to Indian public opinion and highlighted the potential sensitivity of empire films. This contributed to producers shelving a number of planned projects and the temporary termination of British imperial adventure film production during the war (Chowdhry 2000: 43). As examples of the second strand, Webster (op cit: 47-48) cites some wartime Ealing films, such as *The Foreman went to France* and *San Demetrio, London*, 'people's war' features that emerged during the early 1940s, with 'temperate heroes', an emphasis upon the collective efforts of ordinary people and an absence of overt references to empire. Significantly, the examples Webster cites of the third strand, 'people's empire' wartime films, tend to be relatively low budget, state-sponsored documentaries, produced to promote official propaganda objectives. This strand of rhetoric and imagery was not considered by wartime film producers to be a particularly commercial proposition; the few features that could be placed in this category, such as Ealing's *Where No Vultures Fly* (1951), emerged after the war.

Orwell's literary career can also be considered in relation to Webster's categories. His schooling, family tradition of imperial service and adventurism, and his decision to join the Burma Military Police, initially associated him with what Francis Mulhern describes as an 'excess' of Englishness, the 'master-signifier' in colonial conditions (2014: 140-141). Orwell's first novel, *Burmese Days* (1934), registers a critique of this type of Englishness, including its negative portrayal of Lieutenant Verrall, an Indian army and then Burma Military Police officer. Verrall is cut from the same cloth as the heroes of the imperial adventure film. Orwell then shifts towards what Mulhern, not without hyperbole on his own part, describes as a 'hyperbolic Englishness' that 'licensed an uncritical attachment to the good sense of the nation' (ibid: 141). This is accompanied by an anti-imperialism that is often hyperbolic in relation to most other white British writers of his period, but which is related to the politics of the only party Orwell ever joined, the Independent Labour Party (ILP), and which aligned him with some radical Indian intellectuals. Orwell's later literary development, therefore, has to be considered along parallel tracks; not only in relation to other writers on Englishness such as J. B. Priestley but also, as Kristin Bluemel (2004) has argued, in relation to anti-imperialist Indian intellectuals such as Mulk Raj Anand.

CONCLUSION: ORWELL'S DUAL ROLE

For British cinema studies, Orwell can, therefore, serve a dual role. If he continues to be heralded, alongside writers such as Priestley, as a literary reference point for the representations of Englishness in certain types of film, he simultaneously needs to be seen as a limit point for representations of empire in 1930s and 1940s British media. The wartime 'people's empire' film that came closest to espousing the position Orwell adopted when he worked at the Indian section of the BBC's Eastern Service, from August 1941 to November 1943, was the Crown Film Unit's *Morning, Noon and Night*, an ambitious collective documentary film about the British empire that was in production during the same period. Humphrey Jennings was listed as one of the film makers involved in this project. *Morning, Noon and Night*'s lead scriptwriter, Arthur Calder-Marshall, envisaged a section of the film in which 'we go [on the image track] to India, where an Indian [commentary] voice says, "And we too, whatever the differences, agree the common enemy is the tyranny, which is Nazism and Fascism and the imperialism of Japan"' (Calder-Marshall cited in Stollery 2011: 43).

This was the type of sentiment Orwell regularly articulated, and encouraged Indian intellectuals to voice, in his radio broadcasts. However, the BBC context of Orwell's broadcasts, which were designed to convince Indian opinion-formers to support Britain's war effort, temporarily muted his more forthright criticisms of empire. Orwell was challenged by George Woodcock for apparently reneging in his radio broadcasts on the anti-imperialist commitments he had previously articulated more stridently in print media (Woodcock 1942: 417). However, if Orwell's radio work was less radical on the issue of empire than some of his earlier writing, *Morning, Noon and Night* was a step too far for British cinema. It was never completed, partly because the modernised, egalitarian, reformist empire Calder-Marshall envisaged was ultimately considered something that mainstream cinema exhibitors would not want to screen. British imperialism was a blind spot rarely acknowledged within wartime British cinema. This blind spot has been perpetuated by the uses to which Orwell has so far been put within British cinema studies.

REFERENCES

Anderson, Lindsay (2004a [1958]) Only connect: Some aspects of the work of Humphrey Jennings, Ryan, Paul (ed.) *Never Apologise: The Collected Writings, Lindsay Anderson*, London: Plexus pp 358-365

Anderson, Lindsay (2004b [1957]) Get out and push!, Ryan, Paul (ed.) *Never Apologise: The Collected Writings, Lindsay Anderson*, London: Plexus pp 233-251

Barr, Charles (1993 [1977]) *Ealing Studios*, London: Studio Vista, second edition

Barr (1986) Introduction: Amnesia and schizophrenia, Barr, Charles (ed.) *All Our Yesterdays: 90 Years of British Cinema*, London: BFI pp 1-29

Barr, Charles (2005) The Good Companions, McFarlane, Brian (ed.) *The Cinema of Britain and Ireland*, London: Wallflower Press pp 31-39

Beattie, Keith (2010) *Humphrey Jennings*, Manchester: Manchester University Press

MARTIN STOLLERY

Bluemel, Kristin (2004) *George Orwell and the Radical Eccentrics: Intermodernism in Literary London*, Basingstoke: Palgrave Macmillan

Botting, Jo (2012) 'Who'll pay for reality?' Ealing, dreams and fantasy, Duguid, Mark et al. (eds) *Ealing Revisited*, London: BFI pp 173-184

Britton, Andrew and Grant, B. K. (2009) *Britton on Film: The Complete Film Criticism of Andrew Britton*, Detroit: Wayne State University Press

Chowdhry, Prem (2000) *Colonial India and the Making of Empire Cinema: Image, Identity and Ideology*, Manchester: Manchester University Press

Costello, David R. (1989) *Searchlight Books* and the quest for a People's War, 1941-42, *Journal of Contemporary History*, Vol. 24, No. 2 pp. 257-276

Gibbs, John (2013) *The Life of Mise-en-scène: Visual Style and British Film Criticism, 1946-78*, Manchester: Manchester University Press

Gilroy, Paul (2004) *After Empire: Melancholia or Convivial Culture?*, London: Routledge

Grant, Catherine and Kooijman, Jaap (2016) Pleasure Obvious Queer: A conversation with Richard Dyer, *NECSUS: European Journal of Media Studies*, 11 July. Available online at http://www.necsus-ejms.org/pleasure-obvious-queer-conversation-richard-dyer/, accessed on 5 June 2018

Grieveson, Lee and Wasson, Haidee (2008) The academy and motion pictures, Grieveson, Lee and Wasson, Haidee (eds) *Inventing Film Studies*, Durham: Duke University Press pp xi-xxxii

Hunter, Jefferson (2010) *English Filming, English Writing*, Bloomington: Indiana University Press

Hurd, Geoff (1984) Notes on hegemony, the war and cinema, Hurd, Geoff (ed.) *National Fictions: World War Two in British Films and Television*, London: BFI pp 18-19

Jackson, Kevin (1999) Blake, Shakespeare, Orwell ... and Jennings, *The Independent*, 23 December. Available online at https://www.independent.co.uk/arts-entertainment/arts-blake-shakespeare-orwell-and-jennings-1134237.html, accessed on 21 May 2018

Jackson, Kevin (2004) *Humphrey Jennings*, London: Picador

Jackson, Kevin (2001) The Orwell of cinema, *Prospect Magazine*, 20 January. Available online at https://www.prospectmagazine.co.uk/magazine/theorwellofcinema, accessed on 21 May 2018

Jennings, Humphrey (1993 [1941]) Letter to Cicely Jennings, 10 May, Jackson, Kevin (ed.) *The Humphrey Jennings Film Reader*, Manchester: Carcanet pp 28-29

Marks, Peter (2011) *George Orwell the Essayist: Literature, Politics and the Periodical Culture*, London: Continuum

Mulhern, Francis (2014) Forever Orwell, *New Left Review*, No. 87 pp 132-142

Newsinger, John (1999) *Orwell's Politics*, Basingstoke: Palgrave Macmillan.

Newsinger, John (2018) *Hope Lies with the Proles: George Orwell and the Left*, London: Pluto Press

Noble, Peter (1946) *Profiles and Personalities*, London: Brownlee

Nowell-Smith, Geoffrey (1986) Humphrey Jennings: Surrealist observer, Barr, Charles (ed.) *All Our Yesterdays: 90 Years of British Cinema*, London: BFI pp 321-333

Orwell, George (1998a [1941]) *The Lion and the Unicorn*, Davison, Peter (ed.) *The Complete Works of George Orwell: A Patriot after All, 1940-1941*, London: Secker and Warburg pp 391-433

Orwell, George (1998b [1939]) Not counting niggers, Davison, Peter (ed) *The Complete Works of George Orwell: Facing Unpleasant Facts, 1937-1939*, London: Secker and Warburg pp 358-361

Orwell, George (1998c [1946]) Politics and the English language, Davison, Peter (ed.) *The Complete Works of George Orwell: I Belong to the Left, 1945*, London: Secker and Warburg pp 421-430

Orwell, George (1940) The ruling class, *Horizon*, Vol. 2, No. 12 pp 318-323

Rodden, John (2017 [2001]) *George Orwell: The Politics of Literary Reputation*, London: Routledge, revised edition

Rosen, Philip (2008) *Screen* and 1970s film theory, Grieveson, Lee and Wasson, Haidee (eds) *Inventing Film Studies*, Durham: Duke University Press pp 264-297

Stollery, Martin (2011) The last roll of the dice: *Morning, Noon and Night*, empire, and the historiography of the Crown Film Unit, Grieveson, Lee and MacCabe, Colin (eds), *Film and the End of Empire*, London: BFI pp 35-54

Webster, Wendy (2005) *Englishness and Empire, 1939-1965*, Oxford: Oxford University Press

West, W. J. (1987) *George Orwell: The War Broadcasts*, Harmondsworth: Penguin

Williams, Raymond (1984 [1971]) *Orwell*, London: Flamingo, second edition

Williams, Raymond (1979) *Politics and Letters: Interviews with* New Left Review, London: New Left Books

Williams, Tony (2000) *Structures of Desire: British Cinema 1939-1955*, New York: State University of New York Press

Wood, Robin (2002) *Hitchcock's Films Revisited*, New York: Columbia University Press

Woodcock, George (1942) Pacifism and the war (contribution), *Partisan Review*, Vol. 9, No. 5 pp 416-417

NOTE ON THE CONTRIBUTOR

Martin Stollery is an independent scholar who first studied British cinema with Charles Barr at the University of East Anglia in the 1980s. He is the author of *Alternative Empires: European Modernist Cinemas and Cultures of Imperialism* (2000) and co-author of *British Film Editors* (2004). He has published numerous essays and book chapters on various aspects of film and television history and on representations of the non-Western world.

BOOK REVIEWS

The Proletarian Answer to the Modernist Question
Nick Hubble
Edinburgh University Press, Edinburgh, 2017 pp vi+218
ISBN 978 1 4744 1582 8 (hbk)

The term 'proletarian literature' tends to call up images of masculine writing centred on male-dominated work and relations of solidarity predicated on it. The major achievement, then, of Nick Hubble's new book is a significant opening out – indeed, a redefinition – of the category of proletarian writing. Hubble uses the term to refer to a particular way of figuring intersubjective relations of class and gender constituted by fantasy and desire, relations that by their nature overrun stable identities and, in the argument of the book, point forward to the future transformation of social relations. Such a way of thinking would naturally counter-pose it to 'modernism', understood as a bourgeois, individualistic method of registering increasingly complex social relations. Instead, this expanded conception of proletarian literature is here posited as one answer to the major problems that confront literary modernism: specifically, the problem of how to relate the individual to the collective, of how 'I' can relate to 'we' (p. 1).

This is a very intriguing argument, all the more so because the book also revises the historical coordinates of proletarian literature so that it no longer appears as a mode characteristic of the later 1920s and 1930s but as one emerging in the Edwardian period and extending through the long 20th century. The book explores a rich if somewhat diffuse tradition, running through Ford Maddox Ford and H. G. Wells through to Ellen Wilkinson and Lewis Grassic Gibbon; a tradition defined by imaginings of intersubjective social relations that are future-orientated, prefiguring or anticipating, as Hubble sees it, a post-capitalist future. One wonders what the limits of this extended application of 'proletarian literature' might, in fact, be and whether any text attentive to and critical of arrangements of class and gender might fall within its purview. The formal term that seems to operate here, perhaps as a brake on such endless extension, is the pastoral, especially as William Empson understood it in a 1935 essay in which he argued that proletarian literature was a form of pastoral. Hubble identifies a form of proletarian pastoral that captures not the solidarity of class identity but rather a sense of the possibility of classlessness, 'precisely because it did not focus directly on the authentic experience of the worker but on the intersubjective connections between the worker and people of other classes' (p. 7).

The introduction begins this enquiry through examining the utopian socialist-feminist dynamics of Naomi Mitchison's *We Have Been Warned* (1935) and its undoing of essentialist conceptions of the classed and gendered self. The key term here is the slightly awkward one of 'autobiografiction', a device that 'exceeds autobiographical fiction by allowing writers to transform themselves performatively and represent a different understanding of selfhood' (p. 18) through the projection of fictionalised selves. The term recurs in a rather dense first chapter on 'Edwardian Pastoral', which surveys Ford Madox Ford, H. G. Wells, Virginia Woolf and Katherine Mansfield. As a whole, it works against established critical emphases on modernist 'impersonality', instead drawing attention to interpersonal relations in these writers' work which do not so much suspend selfhood as continually reconfigure it through acts of imaginative identification: these 'frenzied and melodramatic reworkings' should inform us that 'self-liberation was never actually achieved by the self but only through the intersubjective relationships which selves formed with each other in complex chaotic performances' (p. 73).

The second chapter considers the reconfiguration of class and gender relations after the 1926 General Strike, focusing primarily on D. H. Lawrence's *Lady Chatterley's Lover* (1928), the pastoralism of which is detected in its concluding images of transformed social relations and is read in the context of the impact of the strike on Lawrence's writing process. The third chapter offers a very interesting reading of Lewis Grassic Gibbon's *Grey Granite* (1935), especially insightful in its attention to voice. The ending is once again here read in pastoral terms, as against the perhaps more common reading of the ending as registering a terminal splitting of voice and consciousness between the 'mythic' female Chris Guthrie and the male, militant-modernist Ewan Tavendale. The possibilities for a proletarian-pastoral approach to enable a move beyond rather stale modernist debates are perhaps most convincingly evident here.

The fourth chapter offers a careful intersectional reading of John Sommerfield's *May Day* (1936) that recognises the importance to the novel of working-class women's desires for a materially better future, an aspect potentially occluded by narrower conceptions of proletarian writing. The fifth chapter, 'Outsider Observations', argues convincingly for the influence of reading working women's autobiographies, and the self-reflection they provoked, on Virginia Woolf's writing of *The Years* (1937). The chapter also considers the ambiguities of Orwell's *The Road to Wigan Pier* (1937), read here as less successful than other texts in deploying pastoral to depict changing social relations, as well as discussing the important role

REVIEW

Mass Observation played in creating possibilities for intersubjective relationships across class and gender lines through 'contacts with ordinary life', as Mitchison put it (p. 192).

The book concludes with suggestive reflections on the relevance of the proletarian-modernist writing of the interwar years for our own political present, and how its unrealised futures might usefully inform a necessary move beyond the ambitions of twentieth-century social democracy. If there is occasionally something a little jarring in the contemporariness of some of the terminology in this book (intersectionality, post-scarcity emotional economy, post-capitalism), this is only to remind us, as we should be reminded, that the insights and ambitions these have come to name are themselves products of the long 20th century, the advances and limit points of the socialisms it has engendered. This is a rich and often quite demanding book which amply demonstrates that the literature of early 20th century, even amid an endlessly proliferating field of modernist sub-specialisms, can still yield fresh insights for our own times.

Elinor Taylor,
University of Westminster

The Duty to Stand Aside: *Nineteen Eighty-Four* and the Wartime Quarrel of George Orwell and Alex Comfort

Eric Laursen

AK Press, Chico, 2018 pp 175

ISBN 978 1 8493 5318 2 (pbk)

This is an interesting but in a way a rather slight book that deals at some length with the not necessarily deeply significant relationship between Alex Comfort and George Orwell and their disagreements during the Second World War. *Nineteen Eighty-Four* does not actually play much of a role in the story other than reflecting Orwell's conception of the dangers of what the state might become. Published by an anarchist press, this is openly not an even-handed study but rather it is on Comfort's side in the quarrel. It has much to say about our present day situation and the evils of government, almost seventy years after Orwell's death and eighteen after Comfort's.

Orwell, at the time of the quarrel, was a moderately well-known literary figure, working during the war for the BBC as organiser of talks to India and then as literary editor of *Tribune*, mostly contributing his splendid 'As I Please' columns. Alex Comfort, born in 1920, was still studying at Cambridge to become a doctor. He was also a poet and novelist and, of course, years later he would achieve worldwide fame as the author of *The Joy of Sex* (1972). He was a pacifist, not subject to conscription as he had lost some fingers in a youthful experiment that had gone wrong.

Orwell wrote a long review in the *Adelphi* in 1941 of Comfort's novel of that year, *No Such Liberty*, which he admired as a novel but did not agree with its pacifism. Comfort was committed to the idea that states were run by psychopaths and that they became even more so in wartime. He felt that by participating in the war Britain would become Nazified. Orwell was hardly an admirer of those who ran the state and his two great future works, *Animal Farm* and *Nineteen Eighty-Four*, argued that if the makers of a 'good' revolution remained in power rather than on a routine basis being replaced by new leaders, their commitment to and love of power would lead to a totalitarian and deeply oppressive state. But he felt, contrary to Comfort, that the state by necessity had to be a coercive force. How otherwise could it enforce measures that would improve the good of all? In his fine short work, *The Lion and the Unicorn* (1941), he had written that, in order to win the war and achieve the support of the population, Britain would have to undergo a social revolution, bloody if necessary. He later admitted that he was quite wrong, although there was a limited social revolution, the creation of the welfare state, after the war. It was almost a payback, it might be said, by the ruling class to the people for having supported the war. Orwell was not that much of an admirer of Churchill and hoped, and predicted, that he would be disowned after the war. But he recognised how much Churchill had prevented Britain from negotiating a peace with Hitler. Orwell was absolutely committed to the war. He regretted that he could not serve, making do with being a member of the Home Guard. With perhaps some exaggeration, he condemned Comfort's position (Orwell was very fond of the sweeping generalisation) as, in effect, being pro-Fascist. And certainly in the very unlikely event that pacifism had succeeded in Britain, the country would have been conquered.

REVIEW

Despite their profound disagreements, Orwell had a somewhat cordial relationship with Comfort, although they actually only met once. He certainly did not prevent the publication in *Tribune* on 4 June 1943 of a 15 stanza poem by Comfort under the name of Obadiah Hornbooke bemoaning the German dead killed by British bombing and attacking Churchill and the political class in general down for their insistence on waging war: 'You've heard His Nibs decanting year by year/ The dim productions of his bulldog brain.' In the issue of 18 June, Orwell replied in a strong 15 stanza poem of his own against Comfort, arguing for the absolute necessity to fight the war. While not an admirer of Churchill, Orwell recognised how important he was for the war effort. 'Which will sound better in the days to come, "Blood, toil and sweat" or "Kiss the Nazi's bum"?'

On 11 July, Orwell wrote Comfort a friendly letter apologising for being 'rather rude' and stating that he thought Comfort was a better poet than he was. He also expressed support for Comfort's anarchist journal, *New Road*, and would try to have E. M. Forster mention it in one of his talks to India. Indeed, Orwell contributed one of his finest essays, 'Looking Back on the Spanish War', probably written the previous year, to the journal, despite its political views. Although annoyed, he didn't even express his irritation to Comfort that the political parts of his essay were cut without consultation with him. The essay ends with one of Orwell's finest poems about shaking the hand of the Italian militiaman (as he describes in the opening of *Homage to Catalonia*) and its final lines 'No bomb ever burst/ Shatters the crystal spirit'. (George Woodcock, an anarchist who would become a good friend of Orwell used 'the crystal spirit' as the title for his important study of Orwell, of 1966.)

Despite their apparent good relations, Orwell did include Comfort on his notorious list of 'crypto-communists and fellow travellers' that he sent to his close friend Celia Kirwan in May 1949. She was working for the recently set-up secret propaganda unit, the Information Research Department, at the Foreign Office. His list mentioned individuals whom Orwell thought should not be asked to provide material that might counter anti-British Soviet statements. In a way, it was a totally unnecessary list as it was quite obvious that most of the names on it were very unlikely to be asked to do so. The issue more turns on the question of Orwell's morality and whether it was consistent with his commitment to decency for him to send a secret 'black list' that could cause trouble for those on it.

In my own view, it was inconsistent with Orwell's general principles for him to have sent the list. His defenders argue that the Soviet threat and evil was so great at the time that such action was justified. His judgement may have been impaired by his powerful dislike of the Soviet regime as well as his bad health. He would die nine months later and was in a sanatorium when he compiled the list. In any case, his short comments on Comfort sum up his attitude towards him and that he was not actively doing harm: 'Potential only [presumably in terms of causing harm]. Is pacifist-anarchist. Main emphasis anti-British. Subjectively pro-German during the war, appears temperamentally pro-totalitarian. Not morally courageous. Has crippled hand. Very talented' (Davison 2006: 142).

Contrary to the author's intentions, this study reminds one of the strengths of Orwell's position during the war. He was, splendidly, the patriotic radical of 'My Country, Right or Left' (1940) who believed that it was a necessary war, despite the evils that were no doubt perpetuated on all sides. That, perhaps, it was even a 'good war'.

REFERENCE

Davison, Peter (ed.) (2006) *The Lost Orwell*, Pinner, Middlesex: Timewell Press

Peter Stansky,
Stanford University

REVIEW

Under Siege: The Independent Labour Party in Interwar Britain
Ian Bullock
Athabasca University Press, Edmonton, 2017 pp 416
ISBN 978 1 7719 9155 1 (pbk)

Under Siege is an important contribution to British labour history. Certainly this reader learned a lot from it and intends, very much under Bullock's influence, to revisit a number of issues and episodes in the near future. There are some disappointments, however. There is little on the ILP's attitude towards the British Empire and how it developed during the interwar period. What was the ILP's response to the brutal repression that the 1929-1931 Labour government presided over in India and what, if any, part, did it play in the decision to disaffiliate from the Labour Party? We know that Reg Reynolds, for example, joined the ILP once it had disaffiliated because of its opposition to the Labour Party's India policy and that he eventually left because of the ILP's support for Zionism. The Labour Party's long-standing commitment to Zionism, predating even the Balfour Declaration, is well-known, but what was the ILP's stance particularly during the great Palestinian revolt against British rule and the Zionist takeover in the late 1930s, a revolt that was put down with considerable brutality? Unfortunately, Bullock does not really explore this imperial dimension. This aside, *Under Siege* is immensely valuable. But what of the special concerns of this journal? What of George Orwell and the ILP?

The ILP was, it is worth remembering, the only political party that George Orwell ever joined. For all the misguided attempts that have been made to reduce Orwell to some kind of Labourite, he never actually joined the party, although he was on one occasion invited to put himself forward as a prospective parliamentary candidate. It was once he had returned from fighting in Catalonia, where he had served in the ILP contingent, that he joined the ILP, on 13 June 1938 to be precise. What does Bullock have to say about his brief sojourn in the organisation?

Of particular interest is his albeit brief discussion of John Middleton Murray and the *Adelphi* journal, a publication that really needs more attention than it has received. Murray was to play an important role in the ILP for at least a few years and the *Adelphi* was of considerable importance in developing both Orwell's sensibilities and his political understanding as well. When Murray joined the ILP his 'Why I Joined the ILP' statement together with a photograph appeared on the front page of the *New Leader* newspaper (1 January 1932). He had joined 'Because I am a Communist. Not a member of the Communist Party. That is a different thing'. Indeed, as an 'English Marxist', he was convinced that the ILP had 'more of the true faith within its ranks – the absolute will to revolution, but not to bloodshed for its own sake – than any other Labour organisation in England'. Bullock provides an extremely interesting account of Murray's politics at this time and of his role in the ILP. As he puts it, although Murray 'admired the Bolsheviks he was clear that their methods should not and could not be applied in Britain' (p. 207).

Murray had already parted company with the ILP by the time Orwell joined. Arguably, Bullock does not acknowledge the extent to which Orwell was already familiar with the ILP, primarily through the *Adelphi*, even before he went to Spain. This familiarity did not, of course, stop him making the ILP's middle class membership one of his primary targets in the second part of *The Road to Wigan Pier*. By the time the book was reviewed in the *New Leader* by Ethel Mannin, Orwell was already fighting in Spain. She hoped that his experience there serving in the ILP contingent would mean that 'he has already outgrown the confused and contradictory ideas set forth in the second part of this book' (p. 291). And it did, of course, although not right away.

Bullock provides us with a useful discussion of the politics behind the ILP's involvement with the POUM during the Spanish Revolution. Within a month of the military coup, John McNair had been sent to Barcelona to investigate the situation. The ILP raised more than £2,000 to assist in the struggle and equipped an ambulance that was named after Joaquin Maurin, one of the POUM leaders who had already been executed by the military rebels. The MP John McGovern also visited the country on behalf of the organisation and it subsequently published his pamphlet, *Why Bishops Back Franco* (1937), that sold an impressive 28,000 copies. The ILP's identification with the POUM was, as Bullock puts it, 'total' (p. 282).

Indeed, on 12 March 1937, the *New Leader* actually proclaimed: 'We Are Proud of POUM.' When the communists provoked the general strike and popular uprising in Barcelona in May 1937 as part of their campaign against the POUM, the ILP stood by its Spanish ally in the face of ferocious attacks from the British CP. Once again, as Bullock points out, CP members actually came close to calling for the killing of ILP members, with the party's leading 'theoretician', Rajani Palme Dutt, making clear that the May events were 'an act of treason which in any war would be punishable by death' (p. 284). As for Orwell, up until the May events he had found himself more in sympathy with the communists' Popular Front strategy than with that of the ILP and the POUM and had actually been on the verge of transferring to the International Brigades. The conduct of the communists during and after the May events finally won him over to the ILP's stance and led to his complete and total disillusionment with both international communism and the Soviet Union. One factor that in particular appalled and disgusted Orwell was the death of another ILP volunteer, Bob Smillie, an episode to which we will return.

REVIEW

Orwell's *Homage to Catalonia* is inevitably seen as part of his Complete Works, the product of his particular genius, but it can be better seen as a book putting forward the ILP understanding of events in Spain. The ILP actually played a part in bringing Orwell's proposed account, initially entitled *Barcelona Tragedy*, to Fredric Warburg's attention. Orwell found himself in close agreement with the stand taken by the ILP on Spain and this, without any doubt, was an important consideration in his decision to join the party.

But let us return to the death of Bob Smillie. Bullock seems to accept that he died of appendicitis probably exacerbated by medical neglect while in the custody of the Spanish police, arrested as part of the crackdown on the POUM (pp. 285-286). This is fair enough, but he does not even mention the contemporary allegations that Smillie was actually beaten to death in an attempt to extract a confession that the ILP was covertly working with the fascists. This allegation was made by his commander in the ILP contingent, Georges Kopp, who himself nearly died while in custody. Certainly, the communists were desperate to manufacture evidence of collusion and were obviously prepared to use torture to acquire it. Nevertheless, in the end, the ILP accepted the appendicitis story, mainly to avoid a complete breakdown of relations with the CP and its allies. Orwell, however, was sceptical. When the POUM leader, Andrés Nin, was kidnapped and murdered by the communists, Orwell sarcastically observed that when his body was found the cause of death would be put down as 'suicide or perhaps appendicitis once again'. And, of course, Orwell had himself only narrowly escaped arrest and almost certain death in Spain. This personal experience stiffened Orwell's determined opposition to Stalinism.

One can generalise this unfortunate failure on Bullock's part to discuss even the possibility that Bob Smillie died under torture: he treats the British CP much too much as if it were an ordinary British leftist political party rather than one that was prepared, when required, to work hand-in-glove with the Russian secret police as well, of course, as covering-up and apologising for the Stalin's regime of mass murder.

Which brings us to the last point: the influence that the ILP had on Orwell's thinking. This is outside Bullock's remit, but it is something of obvious interest to Orwell scholars. While Orwell broke with the ILP over the Second World War, a good case can be made that his revolutionary prescriptions during the war years actually owed a tremendous amount to the politics the ILP espoused when he was a member excepting, of course, the pacifism. And at least in the early years of the Attlee government, he judged it by an ILP standard and found it seriously wanting. Fenner Brockway's *Workers' Front* (1938) seems to have been particularly influential in this regard, although inevitably assimilated to Orwell's own way of thinking. Unlike Orwell, Brockway was in the end to join – or rather rejoin – the Labour Party, receiving in 1964 the party's consolation prize for lapsed socialists of a seat in the political purgatory that is the House of Lords.

John Newsinger,
Bath Spa University

Political and Cultural Perceptions of George Orwell: British and American Views

Ian Williams

Palgrave Pivot, New York, 2017 pp 186

ISBN 978 1 3499 5253 3 (hbk)

Ian Williams comes to Orwell by an unusual route. A working-class Liverpudlian by origin, he was one of a very small number of young British left-wing activists who, in the late 1960s and early 1970s, embraced Maoism – and he became a big enough cheese in British Maoism to meet Chou En Lai and Chiang Ching (Madame Mao) in China as a delegate of the British proletariat. He was expelled from Liverpool University after an anti-apartheid sit-in and subsequently became a railway guard (and an elected member of the executive of the biggest railway workers' trade union). In the 1980s, after dropping the Maoism, he played an important role as journalist and activist in exposing and defeating the machinations of the Trotskyist Militant Tendency in Liverpool, where it had used what he describes as Al Capone tactics to take over the locally moribund Labour Party and (briefly) the city council.

Since then he has had an eventful career as a journalist and author, based in New York since the late 1980s, primarily writing about the United Nations for US publications but also filing regularly as American correspondent for Orwell's old paper *Tribune*, for which he'd been writing for several years before his Atlantic crossing – on Liverpool, on theatre, on science fiction. And, no surprise, his take on Orwell in this collection of sparkling essays is Tribunite – though there are distant echoes of Mao too.

Williams's primary beef is with those writers on Orwell who recognise where his politics came from but give too much credit to Trotsky, which in America means something different from what it means in the UK – a product of what Williams calls 'the mesmerising influence of Leon Trotsky on the American left' (p. 3).

In the US, Trotskyism was the means by which a generation of New York intellectuals – Irving Howe, William Phillips and Philip Rahv, the Trillings, Seymour Martin Lipset, Dwight Macdonald, you name them – travelled in the 1930s and 1940s on long journeys from adolescent Stalinism to a strange cultural hegemony. It was also a staging post for Cold War trade union bureaucrats and state department policy-makers. It didn't matter so much where you began or where you ended up (some became pioneers of American neoconservatism, some pillars of the liberal-left intelligentsia), but you had to have been through it. In Britain, there was no Trotskyist milieu worth noting until well into the 1960s, just Isaac Deutscher and a few others. When British Trotskyism took off, it was largely as a fad of student revolutionaries who lacked the imagination to embrace Situationism – with a sprinkling of Tammany Hall in Liverpool and elsewhere.

So how does this relate to George Orwell? First, because Orwell wrote some of his most cutting 1940s essays for *Partisan Review* and *politics*, the two journals through which the New York intellectuals most attached to Trotskyism abandoned it. Second, because it was a two-way street: Orwell read his stateside post-Trotskyist contemporaries, and one in particular, James Burnham, provided the raw material for Emmanuel Goldstein's 'The Theory and Practice of Oligarchical Collectivism' in *Nineteen Eighty-Four*. And third, because the most notable left champions for Orwell in the US since his death have been two former Trotskyists – Irving Howe and Christopher Hitchens.

REVIEW

Howe (1920-1993), best known today as the editor of the liberal-socialist journal *Dissent* for almost 40 years before his death, edited a volume of critical essays on *Nineteen Eighty-Four* (1983) and was unmissable in the US as a pundit professing the continuing relevance of the novel in the early 1980s. Hitchens (1949-2011), an English journalist who crossed the pond a decade earlier than Williams and became a star of the American periodical press – and, famously, an enthusiast for George W. Bush's 2003 intervention in Iraq – wrote a short book published in 2002, *Why Orwell Matters* (also published as *Orwell's Victory*) that became an improbable best-seller.

Both Howe and Hitchens, despite having reneged on the Trotskyist cause, retained a fondness for the Old Man's critique of Stalinist bureaucracy in their accounts of Orwell's thinking – leaving aside the question of whether the Bolshevik revolution had itself been a disaster. Williams rightly calls them to task on the grounds that Orwell was never properly speaking a Trotskyist and had by the early 1940s abandoned all Leninist and other revolutionary delusions to become a very left-wing Labourite democratic socialist.

Williams writes clearly and directly – and he knows his Orwell. He veers too far at times into 'what Orwell would have said' in the chapters on Hitchens, which now feel like polemics from a different age, and there are plenty of other things about this book with which to disagree. But this is a serious and informed contribution to the ongoing debate about Orwell's politics.

Paul Anderson,
University of Essex

Hope Lies in the Proles: George Orwell and the Left
John Newsinger
Pluto Press, London, 2018 pp 186
ISBN 978 0 7453 9928 7 (pbk)

John Newsinger's new book on Orwell takes its title from Winston Smith's sustaining belief in *Nineteen Eighty-Four* that 'hope lies in the proles'. The snag, of course, is that 'until they become conscious they will never rebel and until after they have rebelled they cannot become conscious'. Newsinger includes this quote not once but twice in his first chapter, which is even called 'Until They

Become Conscious They Will Never Rebel' just to underline the centrality of this point. The subtitle of this chapter is 'Orwell and the Working Class' and it establishes the central plank of Newsinger's argument which is that in order to evaluate Orwell's relationship to the left properly we first need to understand Orwell's overriding commitment to the working class as the only viable agents of socialist transformation.

Viewed from this perspective, what otherwise might seem like a persistent hostility to the left – the disparagement of middle-class socialists in *The Road to Wigan Pier*, the furious criticism of the Communist Party in *Homage to Catalonia*, the satire on the Russian Revolution in *Animal Farm*, and the nightmarish totalitarian vision of the rule of Ingsoc in *Nineteen Eighty-Four* – is actually a consistent defence of the revolutionary agency of the working class against betrayal and oppression. Even those passages which 'his critics on the left take to be his dismissal, even contempt for the working class', are, Newsinger argues, 'his attempt to find a way of explaining to himself, of conceptualising the failure of the British working class to go from being a class in itself to a class for itself' (p. 21). In other words, the central most important experience in Orwell's life was his time with the POUM in Barcelona which demonstrated to him (and to Newsinger reading *Homage to Catalonia* for the first time as a left-wing student in the late 1960s) that a worker-led revolution was possible and that the working class was capable of building a society in its own image outside capitalism and, therefore, becoming a class for itself. For Newsinger, Orwell's politics – including his enduring preoccupation with the conundrum of how British workers could gain agency through class consciousness – can only be fully understood in relation to this context.

The strength of *Hope Lies in the Proles* lies in this unflagging adherence to the significance of Orwell's Spanish experience to everything he wrote afterwards. Unlike his earlier *Orwell's Politics* (1999), Newsinger is not constrained by having to follow a chronology from birth but is able to cut straight to the political concerns of Orwell's maturity – his relationship with the ILP, fascism, the 'People's War', the Attlee government, and the world of espionage – before concluding with discussions of Orwell's posthumous relationship with the New Left and his ongoing relevance today. The result is a crisply-written and jargon-free book with a coherent thesis.

This enhanced clarity in relation to the earlier book is all the more welcome for the fact it sometimes cuts both ways. While in *Orwell's Politics* Newsinger partially excused Orwell's sharing a list of names with the Labour government's Information Research Department (an act which had then only recently come to light) on the grounds

REVIEW

he was 'seriously ill' (1999: 146), in *Hope Lies in the Proles* he frankly admits 'the likelihood is that if he had not been ill, he would have got more involved with the IRD rather more than less' (p. 126). The earlier book faults Orwell for never letting his socialism 'question the notions of masculinity and of male superiority' that he had grown up with (1999: 48), while the new one refers more directly to Orwell's 'reactionary attitude' to women (p. 154).

Indeed, in Newsinger's brief introduction, which discusses his personal interest in Orwell, he makes it clear that he finds sexism to be Orwell's 'great flaw' (p. 4). The book is able to take this warts-and-all approach because of the way that it skilfully draws together all the new research that has emerged in the last twenty years, including security service reports on Orwell and the much fuller picture we now have of the events in Barcelona in 1937, to give us the most complete picture so far of the adverse political conditions in which Orwell found himself. For example, there is an excellent summary of the relationship between the ILP, the CPGB and the broader Labour movement in the 1930s that simply makes the stakes clearer than in any previous book on Orwell. There is also a very good account of Orwell's relationship with the Attlee government, which debunks the reputation for radicalism of that administration and provides much-needed context on that post-war period; analysis that is clearly intended, in part, as a refutation of Robert Colls's claims in *George Orwell: English Rebel* (2013) that Orwell abandoned revolutionary politics for the Labour Party. As such this is a book that deserves to be read by anyone interested in Orwell.

Nevertheless, a focus on Orwell's politics always carries with it the danger of occluding to some extent Orwell's brilliance as an imaginative writer. Therefore, while Newsinger wisely avoids providing close readings of Orwell's novels geared to providing evidence of his politics in the manner that he did in *Orwell's Politics*, he still does not take enough account of Orwell's tendency towards being ironic and playful even when apparently at his most straightforward and plain-talking. For example, Newsinger refutes the criticisms of Orwell made by E. P. Thompson in his essay 'Outside the Whale', originally published in 1960, by arguing that 'Thompson focuses on a brief moment of "quietism" after the outbreak of the war, treats it as the mainspring of Orwell's development, and proceeds to ignore all of Orwell's political activity during the rest of that conflict' (p. 152). An alternative approach, however, would be to suggest that Thompson's claim of Orwell's 'Inside the Whale' (1940) that 'it was in this essay, more than any other, that the aspirations of a generation were buried' (1978 [1960]: 17) is the product of misreading Orwell's irony. Viewed in the context that Orwell was aware at the time he was writing 'Inside the Whale' of W. H. Auden's poem 'September 1, 1939', his comment that 'On the whole the literary history of the 'thirties seems to justify the opinion that a writer does well to keep out of politics' (*CWGO* XII: 105) may be viewed as an ironic comment on the Auden group in particular rather than a dismissal of all 1930s literary politics. This may seem a minor point – clearly it does not invalidate Newsinger's general contention that Thompson's essay is a poor one – but it has wide ramifications in terms of what is arguably one of the most fundamental questions of Orwell studies, which is whether we treat Orwell as part of the broader left-wing literary culture of the 1930s or as an exception to that culture.

The trouble with Orwell studies in general is that the historical tendency of books about him tending to be either pro- or anti-Orwell has worked to preclude balanced consideration of his position within the engaged political fiction of his time. Even a respected general academic work such as Valentine Cunningham's *British Writers of the Thirties* (1988) gives prominence to Orwell but is dismissive of the working-class writers of the decade, while a brilliant survey of the left-wing fiction (including the working-class writers) of the 1930s like Andy Croft's *Red Letter Days* (1990) is distinctly lukewarm about Orwell. As Newsinger points out, this divide has its roots in divergent attitudes to the Communist Party. While this is unquestionably the case, it nonetheless seems a stretch for Newsinger to argue that Thompson's antipathy to Orwell in 'Outside the Whale' (first published four years after Thompson had left the CPGB in 1956) is down to the fact that Orwell's critique of the Soviet Union was too radical in its 'rejection of Soviet Communism as having anything to do with socialism' (p. 151). Might it not more likely have been caused by the dispiriting experience of living through the 1950s, a decade in which the concept of committed art was deeply unpopular within British cultural circles? Indeed, in his contemporary study, *The Angry Decade* (1958), Kenneth Allsop felt able to assert confidently the superiority of the creative product of his own decade over the art of the 1930s, which he characterised as 'the outcome of political cheer-leading and party-lining which produced much unadmirable joycamp poetry and literature' (Allsop 1985 [1958]: 197-198). Thompson was not to know that this judgement would subsequently appear ludicrous to twenty-first century critics; at the time it must have seemed as though the aspirations of a generation had indeed been buried.

REVIEW

However, his anger at 'Inside the Whale' is really a reflection of the fact that Orwell had so unerringly predicted that exactly this kind of disenchantment from activism would arise as a consequence of writers blindly following the Communist Party line through complete reversals of policy geared to the requirements of the Soviet Union and often directly opposed to the interests of the working class. Describing 'Outside the Whale' as 'a sustained and quite disgraceful attack on Orwell' (p. 75) hinders rather than helps our understanding of context, which elsewhere is so important to Newsinger.

The case of Thompson is used in *Hope Lies in the Proles* as the example to demonstrate New Left luminaries' 'determinedly hostile' (p. 150) attitude to Orwell. Amongst these luminaries, Newsinger lists Raymond Williams in passing but does not discuss him further (nor is he included in the index). Yet Williams's attitude to Orwell was quite distinct from Thompson's, as demonstrated by the fact that Williams repeatedly returned to consider Orwell's work throughout his career: in *Culture and Society* (1984 [1958]), *Orwell* (1971) and the expanded second edition of *Orwell* in 1984. While Williams is often critical of Orwell, this sustained engagement demonstrates not the trajectory towards Marxist disillusionment and contempt alleged by John Rodden in *George Orwell: The Politics of Literary Reputation* (1989) but his enduring valuation of Orwell's persistence in tackling the problem of working class consciousness despite finding this problematic.

The only way to uncover these nuances of Orwell's ongoing relationship with the left is to move beyond the entrenched binary division between pro- and anti-Orwell camps. After all, Christopher Norris's chapter in his edited collection, *Inside the Myth: Orwell – Views from the Left* (1984) – a book which Newsinger quite rightly describes as 'intended to systematically denigrate both [Orwell] and his politics' (p. 58) – is quick to point out 'the complicity of both Williams and Thompson with Orwell's '"common-sense" outlook' (Norris 1984: 243). Norris's uncritical account of the superiority of continental theory to supposed British empiricism merely serves to demonstrate the inherent deficiencies of all such binaries (as well as reflecting the late twentieth-century academic context of its production in which all British socialists of the mid-century decades, regardless of affiliation, were dismissed as merely left-liberals). Viewed from this perspective, it makes sense for Orwell scholars to extend the same attention to detail and clear-minded approach to interpretation they bring to their own subject to critics such as Thompson and Williams.

Of course, Orwell himself was far from immune from being 'determinedly hostile' towards communist and popular-front affiliated writers and aside from the problem of his sexism, which Newsinger foregrounds, his casual homophobia also needs to be addressed. However, he was not unrelentingly partisan. For example, in 'The Proletarian Writer' (1940), he wrote: 'I believe we are passing into a classless period, and what we call proletarian literature is one of the signs of change' (*CWGO* X11: 297). In doing so, he endorsed what was in origin the product of communist cultural production. Although, by the end of the 1930s, the 'proletkult' origins of 'proletarian literature' had long been superseded by a general British usage of the term for any writing by, for or about the working class, the genre was still very much bound up with the left-wing circles around the communist-supporting *Left Review*. Orwell's argument in 'The Proletarian Writer' is the basis for the political position he expanded in *The Lion and the Unicorn* (1941), in which, as Newsinger outlines, 'he rejected the idea of what he described as an old-fashioned proletarian revolution' and suggested the socialist movement embrace the 'indeterminate stratum' of technicians and skilled workers most at home in the modern world (p. 19). Orwell's insight was that the classlessness within these indeterminate strata was the consequence of British workers becoming class conscious and, therefore, moving beyond the constraints of the traditional ways of life that had grown up around industrial culture.

Understanding and acknowledging Orwell's position in this period is central to the argument that he remained a socialist thinker. This argument is strengthened not by seeing him as the exception to a prevalent party-line mentality but by including him in a wider 1930s cultural constellation of writers and critics surrounding a broadly-conceived notion of 'proletarian literature', such as John Sommerfield, Alick West, Naomi Mitchison, and even Virginia Woolf in her introductory letter to the collection of memoirs by members of the Women's Co-operative Guild, *Life as We Have Known It* (Llewelyn Davies 1975 [1931]). Thinking about Orwell's proletarian politics in this way, as part of a collective impulse, opens up the possibility of reconceiving the literary culture of the 1930s and demonstrating its relevance to the rest of the twentieth century and beyond.

However, there is still the matter of Winston Smith's belief that 'hope lies in the proles'. If we accept that Orwell's enduring commitment to revolutionary working-class agency was no longer by this time (if ever) allied to a notion of 'old-fashioned proletarian revolution' then it seems likely that Orwell is satirising Smith as part of *Nineteen Eighty-Four*'s black comedy of intellectual complicity with totalitarianism. When Newsinger quotes *Nineteen Eighty-Four* to suggest that, because neither Smith nor Orwell could solve the conundrum of British working-class consciousness, hope in the proles remains for both of them 'a mystical truth and a palpable absurdity' (p. 26), he is striking a false note because this is Orwell consciously commenting on Smith's limitations. This is not to disagree with Newsinger that 'there is every reason to believe' Orwell would have welcomed the workers' revolts in East Germany in 1953 and in Hungary in 1956 (p. 147), but rather than seeing it simply as a vindication of his 'hope in the proles' he would almost certainly have seen it as a grimly ironic consequence of communist regimes' endorsement of a quasi-religious symbolism of the 'Worker' while denying actual workers any agency.

In conclusion, therefore, while Newsinger's book is a valuable clarification of Orwell's politics that deserves to be widely read, it should not be seen as the last word on Orwell's relationship with 'the left'. Future work needs to move away from the idea of Orwell as exception and concentrate, instead, on his importance within a broader collective left-wing cultural tradition that is still very relevant to our twenty-first-century present.

REFERENCES

Allsop, Kenneth (1958) *The Angry Decade*, London: Peter Owen

Colls, Robert (2013) *George Orwell: English Rebel*, Oxford: Oxford University Press

Croft, Andy (1990) *Red Letter Days*, London: Lawrence & Wishart

Cunningham, Valentine (1988) *British Writers of the Thirties*, Oxford: Oxford University Press

Llewelyn Davis, Margaret (ed.) (1975 [1931]) *Life As We Have Known It*, New York: Norton

Newsinger, John (1999) *Orwell's Politics*, London: Palgrave Macmillan

Norris, Christopher (1984) *Inside the Myth: Orwell – Views from the Left*, London: Lawrence & Wishart

Rodden, John (1989) *George Orwell: The Politics of Literary Reputation*, Oxford: Oxford University Press

Thompson, E. P. (1978 [1960]) 'Outside the Whale', *The Poverty of Theory*, London: Merlin pp 1-33

Williams, Raymond (1984 [1958]) *Culture and Society*, Harmondsworth, Middlesex: Penguin/Pelican

Williams, Raymond (1971) *Orwell*, London: Flamingo

Nick Hubble,
Brunel University London

EXHIBITION REVIEW

Orwell-inspired museum installation makes for uneasy viewing

DARCY MOORE

Visiting the Stedelijk Museum with my family, after three rewarding but long days of getting value for money from our museum discount card, was one highlight of our time in Amsterdam. By this stage we were weary and in danger of becoming jaded with even the most fabulous cultural artefacts, but such was the excellence of the curation at this modern art museum we wandered for several hours, delightfully stimulated, making our own paths through the installations and varied pieces on display. One of the most memorable works was a 'wall wrap' created by the American artist, Barbara Kruger (b. 1945) who appropriates one of the most famously disturbing sentences in literature, by paraphrasing from George Orwell's dystopic novel *Nineteen Eighty-Four*: 'If you want a picture of the future, imagine a boot stomping on a human face, forever.'

'Untitled (Past, Present, Future)', an enormous digital print on vinyl, overwhelms the viewer on entering the space. It is challenging to describe an artwork situated on the mezzanine that incorporates two floors, three walls, a lift, steps, escalators, several entrances and exits. One certainly wants to view it from different perspectives but regardless of where you stand, one experiences an omnipresent, Orwellian unease.

After the initial (overwhelming) experience of the powerful quotations in large block text (in both English and Dutch), seeing George Orwell's name and the iconic smiley/sad face emoticons, I started to process that this was a 'site-specific installation' by Kruger, originally created for the Stedelijk in 2010. A placard accompanying the piece explained 'wall wrap' as advertising jargon to describe large-scale prints covering walls and floors in public spaces, like airports or shopping centres. This is the third time her immersive work has been installed in the museum. Each variation is made to fit the architecture of the new space.

Kruger often employs pithily ironic quotes, questions and paraphrases in her art to challenge and stimulate the viewer. Along with Orwell, the notebooks and writings of French philosopher Roland Barthes inspired much of this particular work. The text, in Dutch and English, on the floor and walls, is either black on a white background or in reverse, as are the smiley/sad face emoticons. Kruger frequently uses red borders around black and white images or text in red or on a red band. This particular piece emphasises FOREVER, written in white on a green background. Intriguingly, each step on a staircase has a line commencing with IN THE END and a different ending, including:

ANGER FADES
LIES PREVAIL
YOU DISAPPEAR
ANYTHING GOES
ALL IS FORGIVEN
ALL IS FORGOTTEN
NOTHING MATTERS
HISTORY HAPPENS
YOU WIN OR YOU LOSE
YOU'VE HAD YOUR CHANCE

A few examples of her more well-known provocations in other works include 'Your fictions become history' and 'I shop therefore I am'.

It is clear why Kruger is so widely recognised for her socially aware, conceptual art that both uses and challenges traditional gallery spaces. This installation is awe-inspiring as well as disturbing and one wants to linger in the space, interacting with the artwork, such is the curious power of the experience on the viewer. Kruger is effectively selling ideas, rather than consumer products, employing corporate advertising techniques.

CONTEXT

According to the director of the Stedelijk Museum, Beatrix Ruf:

> The display system allows an open route through the space in which visitors are invited to create their own parkour. The space is articulated through self-standing walls, encouraging versatile interactions between the art works on display. The traditional room-to-room museum experience is turned into a quasi-urban experience where every turn of a corner is a new discovery.

In this way, Ruf communicates her vision for the space which helps to understand why this art gallery is so stimulating. Ruf understands that the way we gather information via the World Wide Web has transformed how images are consumed. The Stedelijk is designed to permit individuals to 'move freely through the space' permitting amazing new combinations. Merging different disciplines, side by side, permits the visitor to make new connections emotionally and intellectually.

As Ruf adds, this approach to curation allows 'people who are new to art to discover how modern art and design evolved and allows seasoned art-lovers to experience the Stedelijk's world-famous icons in a new context'. It was evident within fifteen minutes of entering the museum that there was an energetic, sophisticated curation at work. Ruf is correct in her belief that this new approach makes the Stedelijk 'a living, dynamic institute that manoeuvres between past, present and future'. Kruger's Orwell-inspired piece is a perfect representation of this philosophy.

REFERENCES

Stedelijk.nl. (2018). STEDELIJK BASE opens. Available online at https://www.stedelijk.nl/en/news/stedelijk-base-opens, accessed on 7 July 2018

The Art Story.org (2018) Barbara Kruger overview and analysis. Available online at https://www. theartstory.org/artist-kruger-barbara.htm, accessed on 7 July 2018

George Orwell Studies

Subscription information
Each volume contains two issues, published half-yearly.

Annual Subscription (including postage)

Personal Subscription

UK	£25
Europe	£28
RoW	£30

Institutional Subscription

UK	£100
Europe	£115
RoW	£120

Single Issue copies (subject to availability)

UK	£15
Europe	£17
RoW	£20

Enquiries regarding subscriptions and orders should be sent to:

Journals Fulfilment Department
Abramis Academic
ASK House
Northgate Avenue
Bury St Edmunds
Suffolk, IP32 6BB
UK

Tel: +44(0)1284 700321
Email: info@abramis.co.uk

www.ingramcontent.com/pod-product-compliance
Lightning Source LLC
Chambersburg PA
CBHW080404170426
43193CB00016B/2805